COOKING

Atlanta Style

COOKING
Atlanta Style

**DELICIOUS RECIPES FROM
ATLANTA'S BEST RESTAURANTS,
HOTELS & CATERERS**

by MARGARET E. NORMAN

PROCEEDS TO BENEFIT THE ATLANTA'S TABLE
PROJECT OF THE ATLANTA COMMUNITY FOOD BANK

LONGSTREET PRESS
Atlanta, Georgia

Published by LONGSTREET PRESS, INC.
A subsidiary of Cox Newspapers,
A division of Cox Enterprises, Inc.
2140 Newmarket Parkway
Suite 118
Marietta, GA 30067

Printed in the United States of America

1st printing, 1993

Library of Congress Catalog Number 93-79666

ISBN: 1-56352-096-6

This book was printed by Data Reproductions, Rochester Hills, Michigan.

Cover design by Jill Dible
Book design by Laurie Shock

*To MKN who shows me that living means
daring to follow your dreams*

CONTENTS

PARTICIPATING RESTAURANTS, HOTELS AND CATERERS

103 West

Affairs To Remember Caterers

Anthony's

Azalea

Bice

Buckhead Diner

Chef's Cafe

Chef's Grill

Cherokee Town and Country Club

Chinese Combo King

Chops

Ciboulette

City Grill

Cloudt's Caterers

Coach and Six

Country Place

Dailey's

Delectables

Dusty's Barbecue

East Village Grille

Epicurean Catering

Food Glorious Food

Georgia Dome

Georgia Grille

Georgia World Congress Center

Hedgerose Heights Inn

Heera of India

Hotel Nikko

Houlihan's

Houston's

Hyatt Regency Atlanta

Indigo Coastal Grill

La Grotta

La Strada

La Tour

Lettuce Souprise You

Longhorn Steaks

McKinnon's Louisiane

Murphy's

My Friend's Place

Nikolai's Roof

Olive Garden

Pano's and Paul's

Partners: A Morningside Cafe

Peasant Restaurants

Piece of Cake

Pittypat's Porch

Pleasant Peasant

Pricci

Proof of the Pudding

Red, Hot, & Blue

Restaurant Suntory

Ritz-Carlton Buckhead

Rupert's Catering

Ruth's Chris Steak House

St. Charles Deli

Stouffer Waverly Hotel

Suite Hotel Underground

Swissotel Atlanta

Westin Peachtree Plaza

ACKNOWLEDGEMENTS

I would first like to thank all of my family and friends for their support and encouragement, especially as I came closer to the completion of this project and closer still to the birth of my daughter Rachel! I would not have completed this book without the help of my husband, Mike Norman. He just kept telling me to keep going every time I hit a bump in the road! I would like to specifically thank Jerome, Carolyn and Susan Masters and also Mary Lou Still for coming to the rescue for my son, Blake, as he grew restless with the seemingly endless sound of the computer keyboard.

I wish to express my appreciation to all of the creative chefs and restaurant owners who donated recipes for this book. Quite obviously, the cookbook would not exist had it not been for these fabulous recipes. Thank you to all of the behind-the-scenes people who coordinated the final details of obtaining the recipes, logos and photographs.

I would like to thank everyone at Atlanta's Table who lent a hand – especially Rob Johnson and Amy Connah. I truly hope this project can enhance the wonderful work you all do to feed the hungry in Atlanta.

Thank you to everyone at Longstreet Press, namely my editor John Yow, as well as Chuck Perry. Each had excellent ideas for this book that I never envisioned. Thanks also to Caroline Harkleroad and Shira Levine for all of their efforts in promoting the book.

Thank you, Ed Morse, for answering some technical questions for me on short notice. I would like to thank the Reference Librarians at Atlanta-Fulton County Public Library who helped answer a myriad of questions every step along the way.

And lastly, I would like to thank everyone who was in any way instrumental in the completion of this book, yet whom I may have failed to mention by name.

INTRODUCTION

Thank you for purchasing *Cooking Atlanta Style*, a delicious collection of recipes from Atlanta's best restaurants. This book is truly unique in that part of the proceeds from the sale of each book will be contributed to the Atlanta's Table Project of the Atlanta Community Food Bank. Each of the participating restaurants, hotels and caterers donates food on a regular basis to Atlanta's Table. The food is collected and distributed on a daily basis to more than forty local agencies feeding the needy in the Atlanta area. Through Atlanta's Table and other such organizations around the country it is not an impossible dream that someday, wherever there are hungry people, there will be food to feed them.

When I first envisioned the concept for this book, I knew it could never come to fruition without the participation of a great many people. Through the combined efforts of many of Atlanta's most talented and creative chefs, each recipe was donated specifically for the home cook. I hope you will find the recipes in *Cooking Atlanta Style* to be something you enjoy preparing and sharing with your family and friends, whether you are a kitchen novice or a culinary genius. Although I encountered some obstacles and hurdles while working on this book, almost everyone I called upon was eager to help and ensure that this project would become a reality. *Cooking Atlanta Style*, like Atlanta's Table, is proof positive that the spirit of goodwill and caring is not lost in Atlanta.

Many have said that Atlanta has that perfect blend of recalling the traditions of the past while looking to the future. When selecting these recipes, I hoped not only to represent the current culinary trends but also to bring you some old favorites, many of which have been recreated with an innovative flair. It would be a difficult task for one book to incorporate all of the elements unique to Atlanta's diverse cooking style, but I hope this book will reflect our love of Southern heritage, as well as our passion for quality and excellence.

Happy Cooking!

ABOUT ATLANTA'S TABLE

Atlanta's Table is a project of the Atlanta Community Food Bank, a non-profit, nondenominational organization governed by a Board of Directors. Atlanta's Table was created in 1987 to address the problems of local hunger and wasted prepared food in the Atlanta area food service industry. Atlanta's Table was one of the first projects of its kind in the nation and is affiliated with both the Second Harvest Food Bank Network and Foodchain, the Association of Prepared and Perishable Food Rescue Programs. Funding for Atlanta's Table comes solely from the community it serves. Special fund raising events include the "Taste of the Nation" annual spring tasting extravaganza and auction, the MPI fall "Harvest Gala" dinner/auction and the "Full Course Golf Classic."

Atlanta's Table collects donations of excess prepared food from more than 200 restaurants, hotels, caterers, dining rooms and other food service providers and delivers it daily to approximately forty local agencies feeding the needy in the Atlanta area. The various food service providers donate from 30 to 1,000 pounds of food per pick-up. These donations total over 40,000 pounds per month. The donated food is distributed to soup kitchens, shelters for the homeless, child-care centers, halfway houses and rehabilitation centers.

Recent statistics from the Comptroller General's office indicate that up to twenty percent of the food processed for sale in the United States is wasted — enough to feed millions of people. Meanwhile, as many as fifteen percent of Americans suffer from hunger. Hunger and food waste are problems not only for the needy, but for us all. Only through a cooperative effort of business, religious organizations, community service agencies, local government and individuals can we take significant steps toward eliminating these problems. For more information about Atlanta's Table and the Atlanta Community Food Bank call (404) 892-9822.

Appetizers

Appetizers

Award-Winning Crab Cakes with Three Sauces: La Tour

Crab Cakes with Tomato Remoulade: Hyatt Regency Atlanta

Savannah Crab Cakes: Pittypat's Porch

Crabmeat Strudel: Cherokee Town & Country Club

Salmon Strudel: Georgia World Congress Center

Grilled Scallops on Citrus Relish with Gingered
Vegetables: City Grill

Baked Oysters: McKinnon's Louisiane Restaurant

Oysters Farmer Style: Georgia World Congress Center

Deep-fried Prawn Balls: Restaurant Suntory

Chicken & Spinach Cakes: Murphy's

Marinated Chicken Livers: Pleasant Peasant

Black Pepper Spareribs: Azalea

Roasted Garlic & Feta Spread: Affairs to
Remember Caterers

Fiesta Layered Dip: Food Glorious Food

Chili Con Queso: Murphy's

Red & Black Bean Won Tons: Azalea

Award - Winning Crab Cakes With Three Sauces

CRAB CAKES

1 pound crabmeat
1/2 pound raw snapper
1 teaspoon salt
1 teaspoon tabasco sauce
2 eggs
1/2 teaspoon Worcestershire
1/2 cup cream
1/2 teaspoon black pepper

Place all ingredients except crabmeat in food processor and blend well. Mix crabmeat with the fish mixture and chill in the refrigerator for 30 minutes. Form into crab cakes. Sauté cakes lightly in butter in a non-stick skillet. Serve with Red Pepper, Yellow Pepper and Asparagus Sauces.

RED PEPPER SAUCE

2 red peppers*, chopped
2 small shallots
1 cup heavy cream
1/2 pound butter

1/2 teaspoon salt
1/2 teaspoon black pepper
2 cups white wine

Chop shallots and sauté in 1 teaspoon butter for approximately 10 minutes. Add peppers and white wine, and reduce the mixture until 1/2 cup liquid remains. Add the heavy cream, and reduce again until 1 cup of liquid remains. Gradually stir in the butter. Add salt and pepper. Blend mixture in the food processor for 1 minute. Strain the sauce. Serve over crab cakes.

* For Yellow Pepper Sauce, substitute 2 yellow peppers.
  For Asparagus Sauce, substitute 1/4 pound or 1 bunch of asparagus (tips only).

Serves 6

4

Crab Cakes With Tomato Remoulade

CRAB CAKES

16 ounces jumbo lump
    crabmeat
3 drops tabasco
1 egg
4 drops Worcestershire
1 teaspoon Dijon mustard
1 tablespoon chopped fresh
    parsley
1/4 cup fresh bread crumbs,
    (no crust)
Additional 1/2 – 3/4 cup fresh
    bread crumbs (no crust)

Pick over crabmeat, removing all shells. Lightly toss together crab, egg, mustard, parsley, 1/4 cup bread crumbs, tabasco and worcestershire. Form into 4 cakes. Coat in additional bread crumbs. Pan fry in hot oil 5 minutes or until golden brown.

REMOULADE

1 cup mayonnaise	1 teaspoon chopped capers
Juice of 1 lemon	4 drops Worcestershire
1 roma tomato, diced	2 shallots, chopped
1 tablespoon fresh chervil	2 anchovy fillets, pasted

Mix together remoulade ingredients in serving bowl. Serve with crab cakes.

Serves 2

Savannah Crab Cakes

1 pound jumbo lump crabmeat	1/4–1/2 teaspoon tabasco sauce
1 pound lump crabmeat	1/4 cup seafood seasoning
3/4 cup mayonnaise	1 egg
1/4 cup dijon mustard	2 tablespoons carrots, 1/4″ dice
2/3 cup crumbled biscuits	2 tablespoons onion, 1/4″ dice
or bread crumbs	2 tablespoons celery, 1/4″ dice
1 teaspoon Worcestershire sauce	

Pick over crabmeat and remove all shells, taking care to leave the crabmeat "lumpy." Add mayonnaise, mustard, Worcestershire, tabasco, seafood seasoning, carrots, onion and celery. Mix well. Add egg and bread crumbs and mix again. Form into patties and grill or bake until golden.

Serves 6-8

Crabmeat Strudel

1 pound picked crabmeat	1 cup dried bread crumbs
1/4 cup diced onion	2 eggs
1/4 cup diced red pepper	Salt & pepper to taste
1/4 cup diced green pepper	4 sheets phyllo pastry
1 tablespoon butter	1/4 cup clarified butter
Juice of 1 lemon	1/4 cup dried bread crumbs
1 tablespoon Dijon mustard	

Sauté onions and peppers in butter until tender. Allow to cool. Combine vegetables, crabmeat, lemon, mustard, 1 cup bread crumbs and eggs. Mix well.

Lay out a single sheet of pastry on a flat surface and brush with clarified butter. Sprinkle with 1/2 of remaining bread crumbs. Place another sheet of pastry on top and brush with butter. Make another stack of 2 sheets by repeating above steps. Divide crab mixture and place onto long edges of the 2 phyllo rectangles. Roll phyllo into logs encasing the crab mixture. Score each of the rolls along the top 10 times with a sharp knife. Bake in a 400 degree oven until brown and crisp. Slice through the scores and place on serving tray.

Serves 10

Salmon Strudel

8 leaves phyllo dough	1 teaspoon licorice liqueur
Melted butter	1/2 cup cream sauce
1 18–ounce poached salmon	Salt, pepper, nutmeg
fillet	1/2 pound fresh spinach

Lightly sauté spinach in a small amount of butter until limp. Mix in cream sauce and liqueur and season to taste with salt, pepper, and nutmeg. Layer phyllo, brushing each sheet with a little melted butter. Starting lengthwise, lay a row of creamed spinach (use 1/2), top with strips of poached salmon and finish with remaining spinach. Roll up phyllo dough, folding ends under. Brush with butter again. Place on cookie sheet and bake at 350 degrees for 20 minutes. Cut into 4 portions and top with a dill hollandaise sauce.

Serves 4

Grilled Scallops on Citrus Relish With Gingered Vegetables

12 (10–20 ct.) scallops, seasoned with 1 teaspoon canola oil, salt and pepper. Grill until done. Don't over cook.

CITRUS RELISH

1 tablespoon red onion, diced	1 teaspoon jalapeno, seeded
1 orange, sectioned	and diced fine
1 grapefruit, sectioned	1 teaspoon basil, minced
2 limes, sectioned	1 teaspoon mint, minced
1 papaya, diced	1 ounce canola oil
1 tablespoon each red, yellow,	Salt and pepper to taste
green bell pepper, diced fine	

Combine all ingredients for citrus relish and marinate for 30 minutes.

GINGERED VEGETABLES

1 tablespoon each daikon	1 teaspoon ginger, minced
radish, zucchini, yellow	1/2 teaspoon canola oil
squash, carrot and green	1 teaspoon rice vinegar
onion, julienned to 1"	1/2 teaspoon soy sauce

Sauté vegetables in oil with ginger and season with rice vinegar and soy sauce. Salt and pepper to taste. Leave vegetables crunchy – don't over cook.

To serve: warm 4 dishes and place citrus relish in center of each. Allow extra juices from relish to cover plate. Top with grilled scallops. Top with vegetables.

Garnish: fry 20 mint leaves for 15-20 seconds in 1 cup canola oil. Top vegetables with mint leaves and sprinkles of black sesame seeds.

Serves 4

Baked Oysters

Baked oysters in the half shell are seldom served at home because of the time-consuming task of opening the oysters. Instead, go to any oyster bar and ask the shucker to fill up a box with empty oyster shells. At home, pick over and choose about 4 dozen attractive shells. Scrape away any remaining meat and scrub shells with a stiff brush. Soak shells overnight in a moderate bleach solution. Place in a colander and run through the dishwasher. Now you have permanent natural baking containers. An alternative is to place 3 oysters in an abalone shell (available from cookware shops). When the time comes, simply buy a pint of freshly shucked oysters from your local market. The following is a variety of topping ideas and baking instructions.

To 1 pint of fresh oysters consider adding the following:

1. **Bottled seafood sauce or a blend of ketchup and horseradish topped with a bacon square**

2. **Chopped nutmeat and anchovy sautéed lightly with garlic and green onion**

3. **Thousand Island dressing topped with grated cheese**

4. **Butter seasoned with barbecue sauce**

5. **Minced shallot, parsley, celery, green pepper and tabasco lightly sautéed in butter**

6. **Bread crumbs, oregano, thyme and garlic sautéed in butter**

7. **Hollandaise sauce**

8. **1 pound fresh spinach, 1/2 cup green onion, juice of 1 lemon, 1 teaspoon Worcestershire, blended to a smooth paste**

Experiment with these toppings. Bake oysters at 425 degrees for 15 minutes.

11

Oysters Farmer Style

16–20 select oysters	1/3 cup chopped fresh parsley
6 ounces butter, softened	Juice of 1 lemon
2 cloves garlic, chopped	Salt and pepper to taste
3 diced scallions	8 strips bacon, cut in half

Blend butter with garlic, scallions, parsley, lemon juice, salt and pepper. Place fresh shucked oysters in an ovenproof dish or ramekin. Top with butter mixture and bacon strips. Place under broiler until oysters are just plump and bacon is crisp.

Serves 4

Deep-Fried Prawn Balls

8 ounces ground chopped shrimp	1 tablespoon corn starch
	1/2 teaspoon salt
1/4 onion, chopped fine	1 tablespoon vegetable oil
1 egg	Additional oil for frying

In medium bowl, mix well the vegetable oil and egg. Add the remaining ingredients. Form into dumplings. Fry in 360 degree oil until golden. Serve with your favorite sauce.

Serves 2

Chicken and Spinach Cakes

1/2 ounce olive oil	3/4 cup heavy cream
1/4 pound shallots, diced fine	1/3 cup bread crumbs
1/4 pound bacon	1 teaspoon black pepper
1 1/2 pounds boneless, skinless	3/4 teaspoon salt
chicken breasts	1/4 teaspoon cayenne pepper
3/4 pound frozen spinach	Olive oil, as needed

Heat 1/2 ounce olive oil and shallots in a sauté pan. Sauté until soft and slightly brown. Remove from heat and allow to cool. Pulse bacon in a food processor and set aside. Process the chicken to an almost smooth consistency and add to bacon. Thaw spinach, squeeze dry and add to chicken mixture. Add the cream, bread crumbs, pepper, salt, cayenne and shallots. Mix well. Shape into 8 5-ounce patties. Sauté patties in olive oil over medium heat in a heavy gauge pan until just browned on both sides. Finish in a pre-heated 350 degree oven for 5-10 minutes. Cakes should be firm and juices should run clear. Can be served warm or chilled.

Serves 8

Marinated Chicken Livers

MARINADE

2 tablespoons apple cider
    vinegar
2 tablespoons lemon juice
1 teaspoon garlic salt

$^{1}/_{2}$ teaspoon white pepper
$^{1}/_{2}$ teaspoon dry mustard
1 cup vegetable oil

To make marinade: combine all ingredients except oil in blender or processor and blend for 30 seconds. Gradually add the oil and blend until smooth. Refrigerate until needed.

CHICKEN LIVERS

2 pounds chicken livers
$^{1}/_{2}$ cup flour
1 $^{1}/_{2}$ teaspoon salt
$^{1}/_{2}$ teaspoon black pepper

2 + tablespoons oil
2 green bell peppers
1 dozen cherry tomatoes
Leaf lettuce

In shallow pan mix flour, salt and pepper. Dredge livers in the flour mixture. Heat oil in a skillet over medium heat, adding more oil as necessary. Sauté livers a few at a time until they stiffen. Turn them over and continue to cook about 2 minutes more, until firm but still pink inside. Let cool. Julienne the green peppers and combine with the livers. Pour the marinade over and chill several hours or overnight. Serve on leaf lettuce garnished with tomatoes.

Serves 8

Black Pepper Spareribs

2 racks of baby back ribs	1 teaspoon chili–garlic paste
6 jalapenos	2 tablespoons black pepper
1/2 cup soy sauce	Water to cover ribs
1 tablespoon sesame oil	Oil to fry

In a large pan boil ribs until tender. Cool and slice into individual ribs. Mix jalapenos, soy sauce, sesame oil, black pepper and chili–garlic paste in food processor. Reserve. Fry ribs in hot oil until crisp. Soak in soy mixture, drain and serve.

Serves 6-8

Roasted Garlic & Feta Spread

1 pound cream cheese   **10 ounces peeled garlic cloves**
1 pound Feta cheese   **Vegetable oil**

Toss garlic cloves in vegetable oil to coat. Roast in a 350 degree oven until golden brown and toasted, but not dry. Puree the garlic in a food processor and add cheeses into processor to blend. Spread on French bread or crackers.

Serves 8-10

Fiesta Layered Dip

1 15–ounce can refried beans	Dashes of hot pepper sauce
3 ripe avocados, mashed	1 ½ cups sour cream
1 8–ounce cream cheese, softened	1 package taco seasoning
Juice of 1 ½ fresh lemons	1 cup chopped scallions
2 cloves garlic, minced	1 cup sliced black olives
1 onion, chopped fine	1 cup chopped tomatoes, seeded
1 ripe tomato, seeded and diced	1 cup grated cheddar cheese
	Green onion for garnish

Guacamole: In medium bowl combine avocado, cream cheese, lemon juice, garlic, onion, and 1 tomato. Mix well and season to taste with hot pepper sauce, salt and pepper. Set aside.

Assemble layers: Warm refried beans and spread on bottom of serving platter. Spread guacamole over beans in a slightly smaller second layer to allow beans to show. Repeat with slightly smaller layers as follows: combine sour cream with taco seasoning mix to make third layer. Top with scallions for fourth layer. Add olives for fifth layer. Add tomatoes for sixth layer. Add cheddar cheese for seventh layer. Garnish with chopped green onion. Serve with tortilla chips.

Serves 8-10

Chili Con Queso

1 medium onion, diced small	3 fresh jalapenos, seeded
1 green pepper, diced small	and diced
1/4 cup olive oil	1 1/4 pounds fresh tomatoes
1 1/2 15–ounce cans of Mexican	peeled, seeded and diced
tomatoes and green chilies	2 1/2 pounds cream cheese

Sauté onion and green pepper in olive oil in a large pan until soft. Add the Mexican tomatoes, jalapenos and fresh tomatoes to onions in pan and cook 4 minutes on high heat. Turn off heat and stir cream cheese into the mixture until all ingredients are mixed thoroughly. Serve with crisp tortilla chips.

Yield: 1 quart

Red and Black Bean Won Tons

1 cup (dried) red kidney beans	1 pint water
1 cup (dried) black turtle beans	24 won ton wrappers or
2 jalapenos	egg roll wrappers
1 ham hock	Oil for frying
1 large onion, chopped	Egg wash

Soak beans overnight in enough water to cover. Cook beans, onion, ham hock and jalapenos in 1 pint water until the beans are tender and water is absorbed. Puree mixture in food processor and let cool. Stuff wrappers with bean mixture, sealing each with egg wash. Fry until crisp. Serve with picante sauce.

Serves 10-12

Salads, Dressings and Sauces

Salads, Dressings and Sauces

Couscous Salad: Affairs to Remember Caterers

Tabbouleh: Murphy's

Vegetable Pasta Salad: My Friend's Place

Vegetable Salad: Piece of Cake

Chicken Tarragon Salad: Cloudt's Caterers

Polynesian Shrimp and Chicken Salad: La Tour

Striploin Steak Salad: Ruth's Chris Steak House

Cracked Black Pepper and Roasted Garlic Vinaigrette:
Chef's Cafe

Creamy Caesar Dressing: Houston's

Cilantro Pesto: Hotel Nikko

Fresh Corn Relish with Vinaigrette: Chef's Grill

Papaya Salsa: The Epicurean Catering

Tomato Marinade: Lettuce Souprise You

Texas Sauce: Longhorn Steaks

Mushroom Gravy: Longhorn Steaks

Couscous Salad

1 1/2 cups water (or broth)
2 tablespoons butter (or oil)
1/4 teaspoon salt
1 cup couscous
2 medium tomatoes, diced
1 cup cucumber, diced
6 green onions, chopped
1/2 teaspoon salt

1 cup parsley, chopped
1/4 teaspoon black pepper
1/2 cup olive oil
3/4 cup fresh lemon juice
1/2 teaspoon garlic powder
1 teaspoon Dijon mustard
Feta cheese (good quality)

Boil water or broth with butter or oil and add salt. Stir in couscous. Cover and reduce heat to low. Cook 5 minutes. Remove from heat and fluff. Let cool, while keeping covered. Combine all remaining ingredients except Feta. Check seasonings, adding more lemon juice if necessary. Top with a light sprinkle of Feta cheese. Serve cold.

Serves 6

Tabbouleh

1/2 pound bulgur wheat
1 gallon cold water
1 1/4 pounds fresh tomatoes,
   diced
1 bunch green onions, diced
3 tablespoons fresh mint, minced

6 tablespoons fresh parsley,
   minced
Juice of 3 small lemons
1/2 cup olive oil
Salt and pepper to taste

Soak bulgur wheat in cold water for 2 hours. Drain and squeeze dry. Mix the remaining ingredients into the prepared wheat and toss well.

Serves 4-6

Vegetable Pasta Salad

1 pound box tri–color pasta
1 cup virgin olive oil
Juice of 1 lemon
$1/4$ cup combination of:
   basil, Italian seasoning
$1/4$ cup Parmesan cheese
$1/4$ cup lemon pepper seasoning
3 tablespoons garlic powder

4 cups chopped vegetables
   of your choice:
   asparagus, broccoli,
   mushrooms, red bell
   pepper, red cabbage,
   yellow squash,
   zucchini

Cook pasta al dente. Drain, add vegetables and pasta to serving bowl. Add remaining ingredients. Toss and chill until ready to serve.

Serves 6-8

Vegetable Salad

SALAD

1/2 cup asparagus tips,
cut in diagonal 1" pieces
1/2 cup snow peas
1/2 head broccoli florets
1/2 head cauliflower florets
3/4 cup peas, fresh or frozen
3/4 cup green beans, 1" cut
1 small red onion, sliced thin

1/2 cup diced green pepper
1/2 cup diced red pepper or
1 jar pimiento, drained
1/4 cup chopped parsley
1 cup garbanzo beans
1 cup chopped black olives
1/2 cup artichoke hearts,
sliced
Cherry tomatoes for garnish

Blanch the asparagus, snow peas, broccoli, cauliflower, peas and green beans. The blanching keeps them tender, crisp and colorful. Assemble all vegetables in a large container.

DRESSING

1/4 cup tarragon wine vinegar
1/2 cup vegetable oil
1 teaspoon salt
1 teaspoon sugar
1/2 teaspoon tabasco
2 tablespoons capers

1 teaspoon tarragon
1 teaspoon dried basil
2 tablespoons chopped shallots
1 teaspoon oregano
1 tablespoon fresh basil,
minced

Combine dressing ingredients and mix well. Pour dressing over vegetables, cover and refrigerate for several hours, tossing occasionally. Salad will keep well for several days.

Serves 12

Chicken Tarragon Salad

2 pounds chicken breast, chopped
2 tablespoons olive oil
3 teaspoons minced garlic
2 tablespoons dried tarragon

1 cup mayonnaise
8 ounces sliced almonds, toasted
Salt, pepper to taste

Sauté garlic in oil for 1 minute over medium heat. Add chicken pieces. Cook until done. Let cool. Add remaining ingredients, mix well. Serve immediately or chill.

Serves 6

Polynesian Shrimp and Chicken Salad

3 8-ounce chicken breasts, skinned and boned
1 pound extra large shrimp, cooked
1/2 cup celery, diced
3 tablespoons shallots, chopped
1/4 cup each: green, red and yellow pepper, diced
1/2 cup mayonnaise
1 1/2 teaspoon allspice
1 teaspoon Jamaican Jerk seasoning
1/4 cup toasted pine nuts
1/4 cup dried currants
1 tablespoon sugar
Salt, pepper to taste
Fresh pineapple, sliced and grilled for garnish

Grill chicken breasts. Refrigerate 15-20 minutes and dice into 1/2" pieces. Dice shrimp into 1/2" pieces and mix with chicken. Pat dry diced vegetables and add to the chicken and shrimp. Add remaining ingredients and chill. Serve on grilled pineapple slices.

Serves 4

Striploin Steak Salad

4 ounces butter	2/3 medium onion (Vidalia)
4 teaspoons flour	4 mushrooms, sliced
2/3 cup beef stock	1/2 cup each: green, red,
1/2 head iceberg lettuce,	yellow pepper, julienned
torn	2 ounces snow peas, trimmed
8 romaine lettuce leaves,	1/4 teaspoon oregano
torn	1/4 teaspoon pepper, dash salt
2 8-ounce prime, aged New	6 cherry tomatoes, halved
York Strip steaks, trimmed	8 Kalamata olives

In a small saucepan, combine butter and flour. Heat on high until brown roux has formed, stirring constantly. Gradually whisk in beef stock. Continue stirring until thickened. Remove from heat. Toss lettuces, place on serving plates and refrigerate. Grill steaks to desired doneness. Cut steak into strips, removing any fat. Melt butter in large skillet. Sauté vegetables over high heat until onions are translucent. Reduce heat to medium. Add oregano, pepper and salt. Mix well. Add steak and sauté 1 minute. Add reserved roux and stir well. Cook 1 minute more. Place striploin-vegetable mixture over lettuce leaves. Top with tomatoes and olives. Serve immediately.

Serves 4

Cracked Black Pepper and Roasted Garlic Vinaigrette

¹/₄ cup red wine vinegar	¹/₂ cup olive oil
1 tablespoon garlic powder	¹/₂ cup vegetable oil
1 tablespoon cracked black	¹/₂ cup lightly roasted
pepper	garlic cloves
Salt, more pepper to taste	

To roast garlic: toss cloves in a small amount of vegetable oil. Place in a single layer on cookie sheet. Bake at 300 degrees for 30 minutes, or until garlic is no longer soft to the touch. In cruet combine vinegar, garlic powder, salt and pepper. Slowly drizzle in the oils. Slice roasted garlic and add to the cruet. Mix well and season to taste. Serve over mixed greens or grilled vegetables. Top with freshly grated Parmesan cheese.

Makes 2 cups

Creamy Caesar Dressing

1 green onion, chopped	2 teaspoons minced fresh garlic
1 tablespoon Worcestershire	$^1/_2$ teaspoon black pepper
2 anchovies, lightly drained	$^1/_2$ teaspoon kosher salt
1 $^1/_2$ tablespoons spicy brown mustard	2 raw eggs or $^3/_8$ cup pasteurized eggs*
2 tablespoons fresh lemon juice	$^3/_4$ cup vegetable oil
1 tablespoon steak sauce	$^3/_4$ cup olive oil (not
3 ounces Parmesan cheese (Reggiano)	extra virgin)

Place onion, Worcestershire, anchovies, mustard, lemon juice and steak sauce in food processor bowl and puree. Add all remaining ingredients except oils to the processor and mix again. With the processor running, drizzle oils through the feed tube and blend until the dressing is emulsified. It should look like a mayonnaise. Keep dressing very cold and serve with dry, cold, chopped romaine lettuce. Sprinkle with additional freshly grated Parmesan cheese.

*Due to recent raw egg concerns, Houston's suggests you use pasteurized eggs. They are available in the frozen food section of the grocery store.

Makes 2 $^1/_2$ cups

Cilantro Pesto

3 ounces roasted pine nuts	**2 ounces roasted garlic**
1/2 bunch cilantro	**1/3 ounce lemon juice**
1 bunch basil	**Salt, fresh ground pepper**
6 ounces virgin olive oil	**to taste**

Toast pine nuts. Roast garlic (whole) then peel and puree. Stem cilantro and basil. Add cilantro, basil, pine nuts, lemon juice, salt and pepper to garlic in food processor. Mix quickly. Add olive oil. Puree until well blended. Serve with pasta or vegetables.

Makes 1 1/2 cups

Fresh Corn Relish with Vinaigrette

VINAIGRETTE

1 clove garlic, minced
1 shallot, minced
1 tablespoon fresh thyme
4 tablespoons balsamic vinegar
1 cup salad oil

4 tablespoons red wine vinegar
4 tablespoons extra virgin olive oil
4 tablespoons pure olive oil
1 1/4 teaspoon mustard

Combine all ingredients in cruet and shake well to mix. Makes approximately 1 3/4 cups.

CORN RELISH

8 ears corn, cooked, cut
   off cob
1/2 cup celery, diced fine
1/2 cup red pepper, diced
   fine

1/2 cup red onion, minced
1/4 cup tomato, diced fine
1/2 cup fresh basil,
   finely julienned
1/4–1/2 cup vinaigrette

Combine all ingredients except vinaigrette in serving bowl. Add salt and pepper to taste. Add enough vinaigrette so that the mixture is just wet. Refrigerate before serving.

Serves 8

Papaya Salsa

2 ripe papayas
3 medium tomatoes
$1/3$ cup chopped red onion

$1/4$ cup chopped scallion
$1/4$ cup chopped fresh cilantro
3 tablespoon fresh lime juice

Peel papaya and cut into 1" cubes. Cut tomatoes into halves, gently squeeze to remove water and seeds. Cut seeded tomatoes into 1" cubes. Toss with remaining ingredients. Serve chilled with grilled fish or chicken.

Makes 3 cups

Tomato Marinade

6–8 ripe tomatoes, cut in wedges
1 small red onion, diced
2 cups sugar snap peas
1/4 cup red wine vinegar
2 tablespoon vegetable oil

1 teaspoon yellow mustard
1/8 teaspoon thyme
1/8 teaspoon black pepper
1/2 teaspoon dill weed

Cut tomatoes into wedges. In serving bowl, combine the red wine vinegar, oil, mustard, thyme, pepper and dill. Mix well. Add tomatoes, onions and snap peas. Toss to coat and refrigerate for several hours, stirring occasionally.

Serves 4-6

Texas Sauce

6 ounces ketchup
2 ounces worcestershire
2 ounces jalapeno juice
6 ounces sugar
2 medium bell peppers, diced

2 medium onions, diced
2 medium tomatoes, diced
Garnish: 4–6 ounces cheddar
cheese, chopped chives

Mix in double boiler: ketchup, worcestershire, jalapeno juice and sugar over medium heat. Meanwhile sauté onions and bell peppers in a small amount of butter or margarine until tender. Add onions and peppers to sauce mixture. Mix well and add tomatoes. Serve 3 ounce of sauce over steak or chicken breast. Top each with 1 ounce of cheese and chopped chives.

Serves 4-6

Mushroom Gravy

1/2 lb. fresh mushrooms, sliced thin	4 cups water
2 tablespoons margarine	3 beef bouillon cubes
1/4 cup flour	1 chicken bouillon cube
1/4 cup margarine	1 teaspoon garlic powder
	3 tablespoons red wine

In medium sauté pan, sauté mushrooms in 2 tablespoons margarine over medium heat until done. Remove mushrooms from pan, set aside. In pan, blend flour and margarine over low heat. Stir frequently and cook about 10 minutes to make a roux. Take care not to scorch. In a separate saucepan, combine water, bouillon cubes, wine, and garlic powder. Bring to a boil. Stir in mushrooms, add roux slowly, mixing well with a wire whip. Reduce heat to medium low. Gravy will thicken in 2-3 minutes. Serve with steaks and mashed potatoes.

Serves 6

Soups and Stews

Soups and Stews

Beef Stew: St. Charles Deli

Black Bean Soup: The Coach and Six

Brunswick Stew: Red, Hot and Blue

Chesapeake Corn Chowder with Blue Crab Cakes:
City Grill

Chili: St. Charles Deli

Corn Soup: Azalea

Crab Bisque: Anthony's

Peanut Soup: Pittypat's Porch

Savannah Low Country Boil: Swissotel Atlanta

Seafood Corn Chowder: La Tour

Chilled Peach Soup: The Westin Peachtree Plaza

Beef Stew

2 pounds diced stew beef	1/2 can cream of mushroom
3 pounds potatoes, 1 1/2" dice	soup
1 1/2 pounds carrots, 1 1/2" dice	1 1/2 teaspoons garlic powder
2 cans tomato soup	1 1/2 teaspoons onion powder
2 cans french onion soup	1 teaspoon black pepper

Combine all ingredients except carrots and potatoes in large dutch oven. Cook over low heat, covered, for 1 hour and 15 minutes, stirring once. Add carrots and potatoes. Cover and cook over medium heat for another hour and 15 minutes or until vegetables are soft.

Serves 6

Black Bean Soup

4 cups dried black beans
3 quarts cold water
3 quarts chicken stock
1/2 cup butter
3 onions, minced
4 ribs celery, minced
2 medium carrots, diced
2 green peppers, diced

3 tablespoons flour
1 cup Madeira
Salt and pepper to taste
Garnish per serving:
   1/2 cup cooked yellow
   rice, chopped onions,
   thinly sliced lemons,
   dollop of sour cream

Soak beans in the cold water overnight. Drain beans and cook in chicken stock until tender, approximately 2 hours.

Melt butter in large frypan, then add onion, celery, carrots and peppers.

Cook until lightly brown and soft. Sprinkle flour on top of vegetable mixture. Toss well and cook for 2 minutes. Season with salt and pepper.

Drain cooked beans, reserving the liquid. Combine beans and vegetable mixture and puree in blender or processor. Place bean puree and reserved liquid in large soup kettle. Mix well and simmer until heated through. Stir in Madeira. Garnish with rice, scant teaspoon of onions, several thinly sliced lemons and sour cream.

Serves 10

Brunswick Stew

1 pound each: (cooked)	1 tablespoon sugar
beef brisket, boneless	1 1/4 teaspoons hot sauce
chicken, pulled shoulder	1 ounce white vinegar
1 28–ounce can diced tomatoes	1/2 teaspoon salt
1 18–ounce can creamed corn	1/4 teaspoon black pepper
1 8–ounce can niblet corn	1 1/2 teaspoons tumeric
1 medium onion, chopped	1/4 teaspoon cayenne pepper
2/3 cup barbecue sauce	

Combine all ingredients in a large stock pot. Cover and simmer over very low heat for 4 hours, stirring occasionally.

Serves 8

ST. CHARLES DELI

Chili

3 pounds lean ground beef
6 tablespoons margarine
4 large onions, chopped
4 green bell peppers, chopped
2 tablespoons chopped garlic
1 1/2 teaspoons crushed red
    pepper
2 16–ounce cans whole peeled
    tomatoes

3 14–ounce cans crushed
    tomatoes
2 16–ounce cans pinto beans
2 16–ounce cans kidney
    beans
2 cups water
1/3 cup sugar

In large skillet, sauté onions and peppers in the margarine. In large dutch oven, brown ground beef, garlic and red pepper over high heat. Reduce heat to low and add the onions and peppers. Mix in the whole tomatoes, crushing each one by hand. Add crushed tomatoes, beans (with liquid), and water. Stir well. Cover and simmer for 30-45 minutes, stirring frequently. Turn off heat. Stir in sugar.

Serves 8-10

Chesapeake Corn Chowder with Blue Crab Cakes

CORN CHOWDER

1 tablespoon bacon, minced
1 shallot, minced
1 onion, diced to 1/4"
2 stalks celery, diced to 1/4"
1 bunch leeks (white part), diced to 1/4"
2 Idaho potatoes, peeled and diced to 1/4"
1 ear corn, off cob

1 pint half and half
1/2 teaspoon seafood seasoning
1/2 teaspoon fresh thyme, chopped fine
1 teaspoon chives, minced
2 ounces white wine
1 tablespoon red bell pepper, diced to 1/8"
Salt and pepper to taste

Render bacon in a sauce pan. When crisp, add shallots, onion, celery and leeks. Sauté until tender. Add white wine and thyme; allow to reduce by half. Add potatoes, corn, half and half and seafood seasoning. Let mixture reduce to a thick sauce consistency. Adjust seasonings with salt and pepper. Add the bell pepper and chives. Serve with crab cakes.

CRAB CAKES

1 pound jumbo lump crabmeat
1 tablespoon each red, yellow, green bell pepper, diced to 1/8"
1 tablespoon red onion, diced to 1/8"
1 fresh jalapeno, seeded and minced
1 egg

1/4 teaspoon seafood seasoning
3 tablespoons fresh cilantro, chopped
1 tablespoon mayonnaise
3 ounces bread crumbs
Salt and pepper
Fresh herb sprigs: thyme, cilantro, chives

Combine all ingredients and form into 8 cakes. Sauté until golden brown on both sides. Spoon chowder into serving bowl. Place 2 crab cakes on top of chowder. Garnish with fresh herb sprigs.

Serves 4

AZALEA

Corn Soup

2 shallots, peeled	1 12-ounce can corn niblets
2 stalks celery	1 quart heavy cream
Pinch of nutmeg	1 cup sherry
Pinch of cayenne pepper	4 ounces butter
Salt and pepper to taste	1 ounce flour

Melt butter in a heavy saucepan. Place shallots, celery and corn in food processor. Turn on for 2 minutes, until ground. Add to saucepan and cook over medium heat for 5 minutes. Add flour and mix well. Stir in seasonings; add sherry and cream. Simmer for 20 minutes. Serve hot.

Serves 4

Crab Bisque

2 pounds lump crabmeat	1 tablespoon each: fresh
4 ounces melted butter	basil, thyme, garlic
1/2 cup minced celery	1 teaspoon black pepper
1/4 cup minced carrot	1 teaspoon cayenne pepper
1/4 cup minced onion	1 or 2 bay leaves
3 tablespoons tomato paste	2 pints heavy cream
1 quart fish stock or clam juice	1 1/2 cups white cracker
8 ounces sherry	crumbs

Pick over crabmeat, discarding shells, and set aside. Sauté vegetables in butter on medium high heat for 5 minutes. Add tomato paste and cook for 3 minutes longer. Add crabmeat, herbs and seasonings to vegetable mixture. Cook for 2 minutes. Deglaze with sherry, and let reduce by half. Add fish stock, reduce heat and simmer for 30 minutes. Add cream and return to simmer. Stir in cracker crumbs. Adjust seasonings to taste. Serve immediately. Add 1 teaspoon sherry when serving, if desired.

Serves 6

Peanut Soup

1 1/4 tablespoons peanut oil	1/4 cup red pepper, diced
1/3 cup onion, diced	2 1/4 cups chicken stock
1 clove garlic, minced	1/4 teaspoon cayenne pepper
1/3 cup carrots, diced	1/2 cup natural style crunchy
1/3 cup celery, diced	peanut butter (no sugar)

Heat peanut oil in a heavy pot and sauté vegetables over moderate heat until soft and onion is translucent. Stir in garlic. Toss for a minute or two. Do not brown. Add the stock, peanut butter and cayenne. Bring to a boil, then reduce heat. Simmer, stirring frequently, for 15-20 minutes. Ladle into warm soup bowls.

Serves 4

Savannah Low Country Boil

1 pound fresh white shrimp	6 red potatoes
8 ounces andouille sausage	6 ounces fresh green beans
4 ounces baby corn (or regular corn cut in small pieces	Black pepper to taste
	Celery salt to taste
2 quarts chicken stock	Chopped fresh parsley

Put all ingredients in a large pot. Cook slowly over low heat. Remove shrimp as soon as they have cooked. Set aside. Continue to cook soup until potatoes and beans are tender. Return shrimp to pot and heat through. Serve in a large bowl. Garnish with chopped parsley.

Serves 6

Seafood Corn Chowder

1 pound assorted whitefish:
  snapper, grouper, cod,
  shrimp or scallops
2 onions, diced fine
6 ribs celery, diced fine
1 red pepper, diced fine
1 potato, diced to $1/2''$
$1/3$ cup clarified butter or oil
6 ears corn, off cob
1 pint heavy cream, room
  temperature

2 bay leaves
1 heaping teaspoon Cajun
  seasoning
3 tablespoons dried thyme
$1/2$ teaspoon salt
8 cups fish or chicken
  stock (do not use
  bouillon)
$3/4$ cup butter
1 cup flour

In large pot, heat clarified butter or oil until smoking. Add all vegetables except corn. Cook while stirring until onion is almost translucent. Add thyme, crumbled bay leaves and corn. Sauté until soft. Add salt and Cajun seasoning and cook for 5 minutes. Then add enough stock to cover the vegetables by about 2". Bring to a boil. Add the assorted fish and stir well. Add cream.

In separate pan, make roux from butter and flour. When deep golden, add to chowder, stirring well. Bring to a boil. Reduce heat and simmer, covered, for 10-15 minutes.

Serves 6-8

Chilled Peach Soup

5 fresh ripe peaches   **¹/₂ cup water**
¹/₂ cup white wine   **Dash salt**
¹/₂ cup sugar

Wash and pit peaches. Cut in slices. Mix all ingredients together in blender or food processor. Blend to creamy texture. Chill in freezer to 38 degrees. Serve in chilled cups .

Serves 4

Vegetables and Side Dishes

Vegetables and Side Dishes

Baked Cauliflower: The Country Place

Eggplant Creole: The Suite Hotel Underground

Marinated Vegetables: Piece of Cake

Mixed Vegetables: Heera of India

Peperonata: Bice

Potato Cakes: Georgia Dome

Potatoes Bonaventure: The Suite Hotel Underground

Sweet Potato, Apple and Leek Casserole: Chef's Grill

Dusty's Quick and Easy Barbecue Beans:
Dusty's Barbecue

Epicurean Rice: The Epicurean Catering

Risotto with Wild Mushrooms: Hotel Nikko

Cornbread: East Village Grille

Baked Cauliflower

¹/₃ cup mayonnaise	1 ¹/₂ cups shredded cheddar
¹/₃ cup spicy brown mustard	cheese
1 head cauliflower	Romaine lettuce

Clean and core cauliflower. Steam until tender. Combine mayonnaise and mustard. Using a spatula, coat the entire surface (except bottom) of cauliflower with the sauce. Top with shredded cheese. Place under the broiler until cheese is melted and lightly brown. Serve the head whole on a bed of lettuce leaves.

Serves 4

Eggplant Creole

4 ounces prosciutto ham
1/4 cup olive oil
1/2 cup onion, medium dice
1 cup green pepper, medium
    dice
1/4 cup celery, diced
4 cloves garlic, minced
3 cups eggplant, medium dice
4 cups tomatoes, medium dice

2 teaspoons ground sage
2 teaspoons chopped fresh
    basil
2 teaspoons salt
2 teaspoons fresh ground
    black pepper
1/2 cup red wine
1/2 cup tomato sauce
Dashes of hot sauce

In a heavy skillet over moderate heat, add olive oil, onion, pepper, celery and garlic. Sauté until onion is translucent. Add the eggplant, tomatoes and ham. Simmer for a few minutes. Add basil, sage, salt, pepper and wine. Stir until mixture comes to a boil. Add tomato sauce and hot sauce. Simmer uncovered for 10-15 minutes or until most of the liquid has evaporated. Serve over rice.

Serves 4

Marinated Vegetables

MARINADE

1/3 cup white vinegar
1/3 cup balsamic vinegar
2/3 cup vegetable oil
2 cloves garlic, minced
1/4 teaspoon black pepper

1 teaspoon salt
1 teaspoon sugar
1 teaspoon dried oregano
1 teaspoon dried basil

In a medium saucepan, combine all marinade ingredients. Bring to a boil, reduce heat and simmer uncovered for 10 minutes.

VEGETABLES

1 1/2 cups fresh broccoli
   florets, steamed
1/4 cup chopped onion
1/2 pound mushrooms, halved
1 pound carrots, 1" dice,
   steamed

1 14-ounce can artichoke
   hearts, drained and
   halved
1 cup sliced celery
1 2-ounce jar pimiento,
   chopped

In a large serving bowl, combine the vegetables and pour marinade over.* Toss well to coat. Cover and chill for several hours, stirring occasionally. Drain vegetables and serve in a lettuce lined bowl.

*Marinate the broccoli separately in order to retain color. Add to the remaining vegetables just before serving.

Serves 6

Mixed Vegetables

1 cup each: carrots, green beans and cauliflower	2 tablespoons vegetable oil
1/2 cup green peas	1/4 teaspoon tumeric
1/4 cup minced onion	1/4 teaspoon paprika
1 teaspoon fresh ginger	Salt and pepper to taste
1 clove garlic, minced	Chopped fresh tomatoes

Cut fresh vegetables into a medium dice. In large saucepan, add oil, onion, garlic and ginger. Cook over medium-high heat while stirring until slightly caramelized. Add vegetables (except tomatoes). Mix well and add spices to taste. Continue cooking over low heat until vegetables are tender. You may add fresh tomatoes when serving the dish.

Serves 4

BICE

℘eperonata

3 tablespoons olive oil	2 red bell peppers
1/2 medium onion, sliced	2 yellow bell peppers
2 green bell peppers	1/4 cup water

Chop bell peppers into bite-sized pieces. Heat olive oil until sizzling. Add onions and sauté for 2 minutes. Reduce heat to low and add peppers and water. Cover and simmer for 30 minutes, or until peppers begin to soften. Serve as an accompaniment to any veal or chicken dish.

Serves 6

GEORGIA DOME

Potato Cakes

4 large baking potatoes
4 tablespoons butter
1/4 medium onion, diced
2 strips bacon, diced

2 tablespoons cream
Salt and pepper
Instant potato flakes

Peel potatoes. Dice and boil until soft. Drain, divide in half. In mixing bowl combine half of potatoes, half of butter, cream, salt and pepper to taste. Mash well. Stir in remaining potato cubes. In sauté pan, cook bacon until crisp. Add onion and sauté for 30 seconds. Add drippings, bacon and onion to potatoes. If too soft to form into firm cakes, add some potato flakes. Form into cakes the size of a silver dollar and 1" thick. Cook in remaining butter in non-stick pan 2-3 minutes per side, being careful not to scorch. Cook to golden brown. Excellent served with steak.

Serves 4

Potatoes Bonaventure

2 medium baking potatoes	1 tablespoon fresh chives
4 tablespoons butter	2 tablespoons onion, chopped
Salt, white pepper to taste	fine
1 tablespoon fresh chopped	4 ounces chopped turkey
parsley	pastrami

Bake potatoes and cut in half. Scoop out the inside, discarding skin. In a medium bowl, mix the pulp with remaining ingredients. Press mixture into shallow baking pan so that it is 1/2″ to 3/4″ thick. Cut into 4 sections, remove from pan and brown both sides in a non-stick skillet.

Serves 4

Sweet Potato, Apple and Leek Casserole

5 sweet potatoes, peeled and sliced to $1/8''$	4 leeks, well washed, sliced to $1/8''$
7 apples, peeled, cored, sliced to $1/8''$ (prefer Granny Smith)	$1/4$ cup butter
	$1/2$ cup chicken stock

Layer the ingredients in a well greased baking pan, ending with potatoes. Sprinkle each layer with salt, pepper and butter. Add chicken stock. Cover and bake at 375 degrees until tender, approximately 35–45 minutes. If casserole seems too juicy after cooking, drain off some of the juices. Cut into squares and serve.

Serves 8

Dusty's Quick and Easy Barbecue Beans

4 slices bacon, chopped
1/4 cup diced green pepper
1/4 cup diced onion
3 tablespoons Dusty's Regular
   Barbecue Sauce

1 3/4 cups ketchup
1 cup dark brown sugar
1/4 teaspoon ground cloves
2 16-ounce cans pork and
   beans

In a large pot, brown bacon pieces. Add green peppers and onions and sauté until tender, yet still firm. Add barbecue sauce, 3/4 cup of the ketchup, brown sugar and cloves. Simmer 5 minutes. Drain and rinse beans. Add to sauce along with remaining 1 cup ketchup. Mix, reheat and serve.

Serves 6-8

Epicurean Rice

1 cup uncooked white rice
1 3/4 cups chicken stock
1/3 cup chopped onion
1 tablespoon butter
1/2 teaspoon minced garlic
1/4 cup chopped fresh parsley

1/4 teaspoon ground fennel seed
1/4 cup toasted pine nuts
3/4 teaspoon sea salt
1/4 cup Parmesan cheese
1/4 teaspoon white pepper

Sauté onion and garlic in butter. Add rice and chicken stock. Cover and simmer over low heat until rice is tender. Add remaining ingredients. Toss to mix and heat through.

Serves 6

Risotto with Wild Mushrooms

5 ounces virgin olive oil	8 ounces fresh mushrooms –
7 ounces finely chopped shallots	choose from: morels,
1 3/4 pounds Italian rice –	oysters, shiitake,
vialone or arborio	portobello, chanterelle
4 cups dry white wine	or black trumpets
2 1/2 quarts chicken stock	5 ounces Parmesan cheese
	1 ounce white truffle oil

Sauté shallots in 2 ounces of olive oil over medium heat. Add rice, stir until rice is transparent like glass. Pour in the white wine and stock (about 1 1/2 qts.). Stir steadily for 15 minutes, adding additional stock in order to keep risotto creamy. Remove from heat. Add a little more stock if necessary. Quickly sauté mushrooms in remaining olive oil. Add to risotto along with the truffle oil. Add Parmesan, and salt and pepper to taste. Risotto is best when served immediately. It should be "al dente."

Serves 8

EAST VILLAGE GRILLE

Cornbread

1 cup yellow self-rising
   cornmeal
1/4 cup oil
1 8-ounce carton sour cream

2 eggs, lightly beaten
1 small can cream style
   corn with liquid

Mix all ingredients with a fork. Place in greased iron skillet or baking dish. Bake at 375 degrees for 20-30 minutes or until golden brown.

Serves 8

Entrées

Pasta and Pizza

Pasta and Pizza

Homemade Garganelli with Fresh Tomatoes and Mozzarella: Pricci

House Lasagne: Hyatt Regency Atlanta

Penne All'Arrabbiata: Bice

Pizza Bianco: The Olive Garden

Ravioli with Spinach and Walnuts: La Grotta

Spaghettini La Strada: La Strada

Ziti with Prosciutto Ham, Oven Dried Tomatoes and Peas in a
Wine-Basil Cream: Chef's Cafe

Homemade Garganelli With Fresh Tomatoes and Mozzarella

PASTA

2 pounds all-purpose flour
10 whole eggs

2 tablespoons olive oil
Pinch of salt

Mound flour onto work surface and form well in center. Add salt, oil and eggs, stirring with a fork to mix. Then gather dough and knead for 5 minutes, until smooth. Wrap in plastic and chill. Unwrap pasta, set pasta machine on widest setting and roll through machine ten times, folding over each time. Then gradually roll pasta to $1/16''$ thickness. Cut pasta in 1" x 1" squares and lay out on clean, dry kitchen towels. Roll pasta around a wooden spoon to form quill shapes and set on dry towels.

SAUCE

3 large ripe tomatoes, peeled and diced
3 ounces extra virgin olive oil
3 cloves garlic, chopped
1/2 bunch fresh basil

8 ounces fresh Italian mozzarella, diced
4 ounces Parmigiano-Reggiano, grated

Bring 6 quarts of water to a boil. In large skillet over high heat, sauté garlic in oil without browning. Add tomatoes and basil leaves and cook for 3 minutes. Add mozzarella. Cook pasta "al dente" in boiling water, then drain well. Add to sauce. Add Parmigiano. Toss pasta well over heat for 20 seconds. Season with freshly ground pepper. Serve immediately.

Serves 4

House Lasagne

2 ¹/₂ pounds Italian sausage	12 slices provolone
2 ¹/₂ pounds lean ground beef	12 slices mozzarella
2 medium onions, diced	1 ¹/₂ cups marinara sauce
1 ¹/₂ tablespoons fennel seeds	1 ¹/₂ pounds ricotta cheese
2 ounces licorice liqueur	3 12″ x 10″ fresh pasta
2 cups tomato paste	sheets, cut into thirds

In large skillet, brown the sausage, beef and onion. Salt and pepper to taste. Drain meat. Add fennel, licorice liqueur and tomato paste. Stir well and heat through. Let cool.

Spray large casserole dish with non-stick cooking spray. In bottom of pan, ladle half of the marinara sauce. Place 1 layer of pasta (3 strips), top with half of the ricotta, then layer with half of meat mixture, and top with 4 slices each of provolone and mozzarella. Repeat layers once, excluding marinara sauce as first step. Next, place a third layer of pasta, remaining marinara and top with remaining cheese slices.

Wrap casserole dish with plastic wrap. Cover again with foil. Bake in water bath at 350 degrees for 2 hours. Uncover and bake an additional 20 minutes to brown.

Serves 8

Penne All' Arrabbiata

(PENNE PASTA IN A SPICY TOMATO SAUCE)

3 tablespoons olive oil
1 clove garlic, minced
5 medium plum tomatoes, chopped
1 tablespoon cracked hot pepper

$^1/_2$ cup Parmesan cheese, grated
Salt and pepper to taste
1 pound cooked penne pasta

In a large saucepan, heat olive oil until sizzling. Add garlic and sauté, but do not brown. Reduce heat to medium and add tomatoes, salt and pepper. Cover and cook for 8-10 minutes until tomatoes are very soft. Stir in hot pepper and cooked pasta. Sauté until pasta is warmed through. Stir in Parmesan cheese and serve immediately. Garnish with parsley sprigs.

Serves 4

THE OLIVE GARDEN

Pizza Bianco

1 12″ ready-to-serve Italian bread shell pizza crust

CHEESE FILLING

$^1/_2$ **cup ricotta cheese**
$^1/_4$ **cup Parmesan cheese**
$^1/_4$ **cup mozzarella cheese,**
    shredded

$^1/_4$ **cup fontina cheese,**
    shredded
1 tablespoon onion, minced
1 $^1/_2$ tablespoons milk

Combine all ingredients for the cheese filling and mix thoroughly. Spread filling evenly over pizza crust.

TOPPINGS

¹/₄ cup green onions	**1 tablespoon Parmesan cheese**
¹/₃ cup black olives	**Sprinkle of basil**
¹/₃ cup tomatoes, seeded	**Sprinkle of oregano**
¹/₂ cup mozzarella, shredded	

Chop vegetable toppings and mix together. Sprinkle vegetables over crust. Top with mozzarella and Parmesan. Sprinkle top with oregano and basil. Bake at 375 degrees for 8-10 minutes or until filling is hot and cheese has melted. Cut into 8 wedges and serve.

Serves 4

LA GROTTA

Ravioli With Spinach and Walnuts

DOUGH

3 ½ cups all-purpose flour
4 whole eggs

2 tablespoons olive oil
Pinch of salt

Sift the flour onto a pastry board and make a well in the center. Break the eggs. Add the oil and salt. Knead thoroughly, adding a little milk if necessary to make a smooth dough. Divide dough into 4 equal parts and roll them out into sheets, as thinly as possible. Cover with a damp cloth and set aside.

FILLING

³/₄ pound fresh spinach
¹/₄ pound ricotta cheese
¹/₄ pound ground walnuts
1 tablespoon chopped fresh
   basil

1 tablespoon chopped fresh
   thyme
Pinch of nutmeg
2 egg yolks
Salt and pepper

Stem and wash the spinach carefully. Put in a pan and cook with a little butter. As soon as spinach is cool enough to handle, squeeze and chop fine. In a bowl, place the spinach, ricotta, walnuts, basil, thyme, nutmeg, egg yolks, salt and pepper. Mix well.

Take out two sheets of prepared pasta. On one of the sheets, place a heaping tablespoon of filling every 1 ¹/₂". Cover with another sheet, and press firmly around the filling, cutting between the squares. Repeat with remaining dough and filling. Cook the ravioli in a large pan with plenty of boiling salted water. Drop in the ravioli. They will be ready to take out when they rise to the surface. Drain and serve with a cream or tomato sauce.

Serves 4

Spaghettini La Strada

12 jumbo shrimp	2 ounces olive oil
16 pieces black mussels	2 ounces white wine
3/4 pound cleaned calamari	4 cups marinara sauce
(squid)	1 pound spaghettini
2 cloves garlic, chopped	

In large sauté pan over medium high heat, add garlic, oil, shrimp, mussels and calamari. Sauté until garlic is golden. Add wine. Leave on heat for an additional 3 minutes. Add marinara, and salt and pepper to taste. Let simmer. Bring 2 quarts of salted water to a boil. Cook pasta for 6–8 minutes. Drain pasta. Top with sauce and serve immediately.

Serves 4

Ziti With Prosciutto Ham, Oven Dried Tomatoes and Peas in a Wine-Basil Cream

24 ounces cooked ziti
8 ounces Prosciutto ham,
 julienned
12 oven dried tomatoes*
1 cup sweet peas
1 cup white wine

1 bunch basil, chopped
 fine (chiffonade)
2 cups cream
1 tablespoon butter
Salt and pepper

In a large sauté pan, simmer peas in wine until wine is reduced by half. Add tomatoes, butter and cream. Simmer until slightly thickened. Add ham and basil and bring to a boil. Add warm pasta, and toss to coat. Season with salt and pepper, if desired. Serve immediately.

*To oven dry tomatoes: slice 12 roma tomatoes in half lengthwise and place on a cookie sheet. With oven at lowest setting, bake overnight until dry.

Serves 4

Poultry

Poultry

Chicken Marsala: The Olive Garden

Chicken Filled with Georgia Peaches and Pecans: Proof of the Pudding

Cobb Sandwich: Hyatt Regency Atlanta

Georgia Chicken Skewer with Cross Cultural BBQ Sauce: Partners
A Morningside Cafe

Grilled Duck Steak with Mango Salsa: Azalea

Peanut Chicken: Anthony's

Stuffed Chicken Breast with Champagne Sauce: La Tour

Stuffed Chicken Breast with Dill Butter Sauce: Houlihan's

Chicken Marsala

4 chicken breast halves, boned and skinned	4 tablespoons butter or margarine
1/4 cup flour	4 tablespoons oil
1/2 teaspoon salt	1/2 cup fresh mushrooms, sliced
1/4 teaspoon pepper	
1/2 teaspoon oregano, dried	1/2 cup Marsala wine

Pound chicken to 1/4" thickness between 2 sheets of plastic wrap. Combine flour, salt, pepper and oregano and mix well. Heat the oil and butter in a heavy skillet over medium high heat. Dredge chicken in flour mixture. Cook chicken until lightly browned on first side (about 2 minutes). Turn chicken and add mushrooms around the chicken pieces. Cook about 2 minutes more, until lightly browned. Stir the mushrooms. Add wine around chicken. Cover, simmer 10 minutes. Serve with pasta.

Serves 4

Chicken Filled With Georgia Peaches and Pecans

5 8–ounce chicken breasts, boned and skinned	1/4 cup diced pecans
3 peaches, peeled	1/2 ounce Southern bourbon
	1/4 cup bread crumbs

Pound chicken between 2 pieces of plastic wrap until doubled in size. Cut the peeled peaches into wedges and mix with remaining ingredients. Divide the filling among the 5 chicken breasts and place 1/5 of the mixture in the center of each. Roll up like a jelly roll, folding edges over so that the filling doesn't run out. Season with salt and your choice of fresh herbs. Bake at 350 degrees for 20-25 minutes. When the chicken has cooled down, slice into 8 slices and serve with grilled sweet potatoes and marinated sugar snap peas.

Serves 5

Cobb Sandwich

4 6– to 8–ounce chicken breasts boneless and skinless	4 ounces sun sprouts
Mayonnaise	1 cup bleu cheese, crumbled
8 strips cooked bacon	8 slices whole wheat beer
8 leaves bibb lettuce	bread or other bread of
4 slices tomato	your choice

Season chicken breasts with salt and pepper. Grill until done. Spread mayonnaise on bread. Top with grilled chicken, bacon, lettuce, tomato, sprouts and bleu cheese. Serve with chips.

Serves 4

Georgia Chicken Skewer With Cross Cultural BBQ Sauce

CROSS CULTURAL BBQ SAUCE

1/2 cup Vidalia or Texas onion, diced fine	1/4 cup lemon juice
1 tablespoon peanut oil	2 tablespoons dark brown sugar
2 cups ketchup	4 ounces hoisin sauce
1 tablespoon chipotles or canned smoked jalapenos, diced fine	1 ounce fresh ginger, minced
1/4 cup dry white wine	1 tablespoon lemongrass or lemon zest to taste
3/4 cup white vinegar	1 tablespoon minced garlic
1/4 cup red vinegar	Pepper to taste

Sauté onions in a heavy enamel pot until slightly brown. Add remaining ingredients and incorporate well. Bring to a boil; immediately reduce heat to a low simmer. Simmer for approximately 20-30 minutes. Set aside for use when grilling skewers.

CHICKEN SKEWERS

4 6- to 8-ounce boneless, skinless chicken breasts	4 long bamboo skewers
2 Vidalia or Texas onions	1 sliced jalapeno
2 red sweet Holland peppers	1/2 cup pineapple juice
2 sweet potatoes	2 tablespoons peanut oil
	1/2 cup BBQ sauce

Marinate bamboo skewers overnight in the pineapple juice and sliced jalapeno. Cook sweet potatoes until almost done and slice into thick wedges. Cut chicken breasts into morsels appropriate for skewers. Do the same with the peppers, potato and onion (keep onion in thick chunks). Rub prepared skewers with peanut oil and assemble, alternating ingredients. Brush grill with peanut oil. Grill skewers, basting with the BBQ sauce several times. Serve brochettes on a warm plate with a small cup of BBQ sauce on the side.

Serves 4

Grilled Duck Steak With Mango Salsa

4 double (12–14 ounce)
   boneless duck breasts
1 ripe mango
1 ripe tomato
1 lime

Fresh chopped cilantro
   and basil to taste
2 tablespoons olive oil
1 tablespoon balsamic vinegar
Salt and pepper to taste

Trim excess fat from duck breasts and score the remaining skin on the breasts. Reserve ready for the grill. Peel mango and slice, then dice the fruit into small squares. Dice the tomato similarly and place in a bowl with the mango. Grate the green skin of the lime and add to the mango and tomato. Section the lime fillets, discard the pits and skin, and add to the bowl. Season with salt, pepper, cilantro and basil. Add olive oil and vinegar. Grill duck breasts to medium rare. Top with salsa.

Serves 4

ANTHONY'S

Peanut Chicken

4 chicken breasts, boneless,
  skinless, pounded to $1/4''$
2 cups ground blanched
  peanuts
$1/4$ cup flour
2 large eggs, beaten
1 tablespoon vegetable oil
6 cloves garlic, minced

1 small onion, diced
Pinch crushed red pepper
1 tablespoon lemon juice
1 tablespoon soy sauce
12 ounce crunchy peanut
  butter
1 $1/2$ tablespoons sugar
1 cup coconut milk

Season chicken with salt and pepper, dredge in flour, dip into the beaten eggs and dredge in ground peanuts. Place in greased pan and bake at 350 degrees 8 minutes per side, or until done.

Meanwhile, prepare sauce: sauté garlic, onion and red pepper in oil until onion is translucent. Add peanut butter, soy sauce, lemon juice and sugar. Heat through. Add coconut milk and bring to a simmer. Adjust seasonings. If sauce is too thick, add a little water. Serve over chicken.

Serves 4

Stuffed Chicken Breast With Champagne Sauce

5 8–ounce boneless, skinless chicken breasts	4 ounces heavy cream
	1 teaspoon Worcestershire
2 tablespoons butter	1 teaspoon tabasco
1/2 onion, diced	Juice of 1/2 lemon
1 small carrot, diced	4 shallots, chopped
1/2 red pepper, diced	1/2 bottle champagne
1 rib celery, diced	1 pint heavy cream
3 cups chicken broth	1 stick butter
1 egg	Salt and pepper

Sauté onion, carrot and celery in butter. Cool in refrigerator for 15 minutes.

Prepare chicken mousse stuffing: dice 1 chicken breast. In food processor bowl place diced chicken, egg, 4 ounces cream, Worcestershire, tabasco, lemon juice and pinch of salt and pepper. Process for 3 minutes. Fold in sautéed vegetables and diced red pepper. Pound chicken breasts, divide chicken mousse into 4 equal parts. Place mousse in center of each breast and fold over. Wrap in plastic wrap separately and refrigerate for 30 minutes. Grill chicken lightly to mark off. Place in casserole dish with broth and bake at 400 degrees for 10-15 minutes or until done.

To make champagne sauce: Finely chop shallots, sauté until soft in a little clarified butter or oil. Add the champagne. Reduce by 3/4 and add the cream. Reduce by 1/2. Add the stick of butter. Cook for a few minutes, stirring. Strain the sauce, add salt and pepper. Allow baked chicken to sit for 10 minutes. Top with sauce.

Serves 4

Stuffed Chicken Breast With Dill Butter Sauce

STUFFED CHICKEN

6 6–ounce boneless, skinless chicken breasts	1 1/2 teaspoons ground white pepper
8 ounces herb & garlic cream cheese	3 eggs
3/4 cup all–purpose flour	2 tablespoons salad oil
1 1/2 teaspoons seasoned salt	Fresh white bread crumbs
	Clarified butter

Place chicken between sheets of wax paper and flatten to 1/4". Place on work surface skinned side down. Put 2 tablespoons of cheese in center of each. Fold chicken over cheese completely. Cover with plastic wrap. Chill for at least 1 hour.

In small bowl, combine flour, seasoned salt and pepper. Mix well. Dredge chicken lightly, coating evenly. Shake off excess. Prepare egg wash by rapidly whisking eggs and oil in a bowl. Dip chicken in wash and drain well. Coat chicken in as many bread crumbs as needed to cover. In large saucepan on medium heat, melt enough butter to cover. When hot add chicken and brown on first side until golden. Turn chicken over and place in oven-proof skillet in 375 degree oven. Bake 8-10 minutes, or until second side is golden brown. Remove chicken from skillet and drain well to remove any excess fat. Place on serving platter and serve with watercress. Ladle 2 ounces of Dill Butter Sauce on top and serve immediately.

DILL BUTTER SAUCE

1 tablespoon finely minced shallots	3/4 teaspoon seasoned salt
3/4 cup chablis dry white wine	1 1/2 tablespoon fresh strained lemon juice
1 cup heavy whipping cream	1 1/2 tablespoons fresh dill
1/2 teaspoon Worcestershire	1 pound unsalted butter
1/4 teaspoon tabasco	

Combine the shallots and wine in a medium saucepan over medium heat. Reduce mixture to 2 tablespoons and add the cream, stirring well. Bring to simmer. Add all of the seasonings. Continue cooking, stirring often, until the sauce is slightly thickened and reduced to 1/2 cup. Cut the butter into small pieces and whisk into sauce, a few pieces at a time, over low heat. Do not allow sauce to boil. Keep warm until ready to serve over stuffed chicken.

Serves 6

Meat

Meat

Grilled Sirloin Steak with Elephant Garlic Crust: Georgia Dome

Roast Prime Tenderloin with Mixed Mushroom Sauté: Chops

Spicy Szechuan Beef: Chinese Combo King

Marinated Veal Chops with Vidalia Onion Compote: The
Ritz-Carlton Buckhead

Sautéed Veal Medallions with Chive Sauce and Vegetable Ravioli:
The Hedgerose Heights Inn

Lamb Shank Osso Buco: Swissôtel Atlanta

Grilled Sirloin Steak With Elephant Garlic Crust

4 6– to 8–ounce sirloin steaks	**¹/₈ teaspoon crushed red pepper**
1 bulb elephant garlic, diced	**1 cup bread crumbs**
¹/₂ medium onion, diced	**3 tablespoons olive oil**

Heat 1 tablespoon oil in a sauté pan. Add diced onion, cook for 1 minute over medium heat, then add elephant garlic. Cook for 3 minutes more over low heat. Be careful not to burn garlic. Remove from heat and cool. In a food processor, blend bread crumbs, garlic mixture, 2 tablespoons olive oil and red pepper for 10 seconds. Season steaks and grill to preferred doneness. Spread garlic mixture evenly over the grilled steaks and brown under a broiler for 15-20 seconds or until golden brown. Serve immediately with potato cakes.

Serves 4

Roast Prime Tenderloin With Mixed Mushroom Sauté

2 pounds center cut tenderloin, close trim with some exterior fat remaining
Assorted mushrooms — any or all of the following, 4 ounces each: domestic, shiitake, oyster, morel, porcini, chanterelle or trumpets
Salt and pepper
1 ounce extra virgin olive oil
1 ounce butter
1 shallot, diced fine
1/4 cup dry sherry
fresh chopped parsley for garnish

Season tenderloin liberally with salt and pepper. Sear well on all sides in a smoking hot pan. Roast in a 400 degree oven for 10-15 minutes for medium rare. Remove from pan and let rest 10 minutes before slicing.

Remove stems from shiitake, oyster and domestic mushrooms. Slice 1/4" thick. Cut porcini, morels and chanterelles a little smaller. Stem trumpets and cut in half. Preheat a large sauté pan. Add oil and butter. When butter foams add shallot, domestic, shiitake and oysters. Sauté 2-3 minutes. Add chanterelles, porcinis and morels. Toss, then cool for a few minutes. Splash with sherry and season with salt and pepper. Add trumpets. Remove from heat. Serve over tenderloin and top with parsley.

Serves 4

Spicy Szechuan Beef

1 pound beef (London Broil)	2 teaspoons sherry
1 small piece fresh ginger	4 cups oil
1 tablespoon soy sauce	1 bunch scallions
1 teaspoon cornstarch	1 tablespoon sesame oil
1 egg, slightly beaten	1 teaspoon fresh jalapeno
1 teaspoon salt	or crushed red pepper

Cut beef into thin shreds, marinate with half of the soy sauce, all of the cornstarch and egg. Cut scallions slantwise into small pieces. Shred ginger. Heat 4 cups oil and place beef into hot oil for just 10 seconds and remove. In 3 tablespoons reserved boiling oil, stir fry ginger and jalapeno or crushed red pepper briefly. Add scallions, salt, beef shreds, remaining soy sauce and sherry. Stir fry quickly over high heat. Add sesame oil. Remove from heat and serve over rice or chinese noodles.

Serves 4

Marinated Veal Chops With Vidalia Onion Compote

4 12–ounce veal chops

MARINADE

2 cloves garlic, chopped
1/3 cup balsamic vinegar
1/2 cup olive oil
Salt and pepper

1/3 cup white wine
1 sprig rosemary
1 sprig thyme

Whisk marinade ingredients together. Marinate meat, covered in refrigerator, for at least 2 hours.

COMPOTE

1/4 pound bacon
1/2 pound Vidalia onions
2 tablespoons water

2 tablespoons sugar
4 tablespoons sherry vinegar
Salt and pepper

Cut bacon into small strips. Chop onion and set aside. Sauté bacon in skillet on high heat until almost crisp. Drain fat. Add onion and continue cooking over medium high heat with the bacon until the onion is almost translucent. In saucepan, combine sugar and water. Boil until mixture caramelizes. Add vinegar and reduce by half. Add onion mixture and bring to a boil. Place in a small casserole dish and cover with parchment paper. Bake in a 350 degree oven for 20 minutes. While compote is cooking, grill chops to desired temperature. Place veal chop on plate. Top with compote and serve with your favorite vegetables.

Serves 4

Sautéed Veal Medallions With Chive Sauce and Vegetable Ravioli

VEGETABLE RAVIOLI

1/4 cup each (diced fine) red and green pepper, zucchini, eggplant	10 fresh basil leaves, minced fine
1/4 cup olive oil	2 tablespoons bread crumbs
1 clove garlic, minced	12 round won ton wrappers

Make ravioli first. Sauté the vegetables, basil and garlic in oil until cooked but slightly crisp. Add the bread crumbs and season with salt and pepper. Form ravioli by placing a few teaspoons of the filling in the center of each circle. Fold in half to make a crescent, moisten the edges and crimp closed. Poach in boiling salted water for 3 minutes, remove and drain well.

VEAL MEDALLIONS WITH CHIVE SAUCE

1 1/2 pounds veal tenderloin, cut into 12 medallions	4 tablespoons tomato, peeled seeded and diced
3 tablespoons clarified butter	4 tablespoons minced fresh chives
1/2 cup white wine	24 asparagus spears, steamed
1/4 cup vermouth	4 tomatoes, peeled, seeded, and chopped
1 cup heavy cream	
1/4 cup demiglace	
2 tablespoons unsalted butter	

Season veal with salt and pepper, dust lightly in flour and sauté in clarified butter over high heat until done. Remove meat from pan, set aside and keep warm. Add wine, vermouth and demiglace to pan and reduce by half. Mixture should be thick enough to coat the back of a spoon. Whisk in the butter, bit by bit. Add cream and stir well. Then add the 4 tablespoons each of tomato and chives. Season with salt and pepper to taste.

To serve: Divide the 4 chopped tomatoes among the plates and place three vegetable ravioli on top. Fan eight asparagus tips out from the center, top with three sautéed veal medallions and dress with the sauce.

Serves 4

SWISSÔTEL

Lamb Shank Osso Buco

4 12- to 14-ounce lamb shanks	2 sprigs thyme
1 cup white wine	1 sprig rosemary
2 cloves garlic, crushed	1/2 cup olive oil
1 carrot, chopped	Flour for dredge
1 stalk celery, chopped	2 cups canned or fresh
1/2 large onion, chopped	beef or veal stock
1 32-ounce can Italian plum	Garnish: lemon peel,
tomatoes	parsley, sweet garlic

Salt and pepper the lamb. Dredge in flour. Brown lamb on both sides in the olive oil in a large skillet. When lamb has browned, transfer to a plate and keep warm.

In the large skillet, add the vegetables, herbs and tomatoes. Cook, while stirring, until the mixture just begins to caramelize. Add wine. Cook over medium heat until the wine has reduced by half. Place lamb, vegetable mixture and stock in large covered casserole dish and bake at 350 degrees for 2 to 2 1/2 hours, or until lamb is falling off of the bone. Serve with rice or risotto. Garnish with julienned lemon peel, chopped parsley and sweet (blanched) garlic.

Serves 4

Fish and Shellfish

Fish and Shellfish

Halibut with Salsa and Mango: The Westin Peachtree Plaza

Duo of Smoked Salmon and Scallop Mousses with Tomato and Chive
Cream Sauce: Nikolai's Roof

Loin of Lightly Smoked Salmon with Roasted Pepper Vinaigrette
and Cilantro Pesto: Pano's and Paul's

Mille Feuilles of Salmon in Phyllo with Vegetables:
Nikolai's Roof

Paupiettes of Pacifique Salmon with Vegetables: 103 West

Seafood Sausage with Dill Sauce: Ciboulette

"Barbecued" Shrimp: Ruth's Chris Steak House

Chipotle Spiced Shrimp with a Salad of Fennel and Radicchio:
Buckhead Diner

Shrimp Cristoforo: The Olive Garden

Swordfish Au Poivre: Dailey's

Tuna Steaks with Gwo Ba on a Pineapple Vinaigrette: Georgia Dome

Halibut With Salsa and Mango

4 6–ounce halibut fillets	Tabasco to taste
4 cups water	2 teaspoons each: (chopped)
2 cups white wine	cilantro, green olives,
Salt and pepper	red pepper, green pepper,
2 teaspoons chopped shallots	tomato
1 ¹/₂ teaspoons chopped	1 cup tomato juice
jalapenos	Juice of 2 lemons
2 dashes olive oil	2 mangoes

Salt and pepper the halibut and poach in the water and wine, covered, until cooked and tender. Mix all remaining ingredients together except mango. Add salt and pepper to taste and chill. Peel mangoes, cut in 4 wedges each. Cut wedges into a fan design. Arrange mango, salsa and halibut on plate. Serve warm.

Serves 4

Duo of Smoked Salmon and Scallop Mousses With Tomato and Chive Cream Sauce

1 pound smoked salmon	1 quart fish stock
4 whole eggs	2 cups white wine
2 egg whites	2 cups whipping cream
1 pint whipping cream	1/2 pound butter
1 pound sea scallops	1/2 bunch chives,
4 egg whites	chopped fine
1 pint whipping cream	2 tomatoes, diced

Puree the smoked salmon in a food processor with the 4 eggs and 2 egg whites for 2-3 minutes, or until consistency is smooth. Place the mixture in a mixing bowl. Add the cream little by little with a spatula. Season to taste with salt and pepper. Repeat procedure with sea scallops, 4 egg whites and whipping cream. Refrigerate 1 hour.

Butter 32 individual molds and fill 16 with salmon mousse, 16 with scallop mousse. Cook them in a double boiler with a water bath for 15-20 minutes in a 350 degree oven. Place the fish stock and the white wine into a saucepan and boil to reduce by two-thirds. Add the cream and continue boiling to reduce by one-third. Whisk in the butter little by little. Season with salt and pepper. Add the chives and tomato. Spoon some of the sauce onto each plate. Place 2 of each mousse atop and serve.

Serves 8

113

Loin of Lightly Smoked Salmon With Roasted Pepper Vinaigrette and Cilantro Pesto

4 6–ounce loins of salmon
Teriyaki sauce
4 ounces cilantro leaves
1 clove garlic
2 ounces Parmesan cheese
2 ounces olive oil
6 ounces pine nuts

2 medium bell peppers,
    oven roasted
2 ounces rice vinegar
4 ounces olive oil
Pinch cayenne
Salt and pepper
4 sheets rice paper

Brush the salmon with teriyaki sauce and smoke for 4-5 minutes in a stove top smoker. Meanwhile prepare the pesto. In blender or food processor, combine the cilantro, garlic, Parmesan cheese, 2 ounces olive oil and pine nuts. Puree ingredients until smooth. Place in bowl and set aside.

Prepare the roasted pepper vinaigrette by combining the roasted and peeled bell peppers, rice vinegar, 4 ounces olive oil and cayenne in processor and puree until smooth. Place in bowl and set aside. Take four sheets of rice paper and lay them side by side on a dampened towel. Cover with another towel. Season the salmon with salt and pepper. Cover with cilantro pesto and roll the rice paper around the loin to enclose. Heat additional olive oil in a non-stick pan, add the salmon rolls and cook on both sides until brown and crisp.

To serve, slice the salmon into three equal pieces. Place on a plate and drizzle the roasted pepper vinaigrette around. Spoon the pesto on top. Garnish with additional cilantro leaves.

Serves 4

Mille Feuilles of Salmon in Phyllo With Vegetables

2 pounds fillet of salmon	3 tablespoons tarragon
1 package phyllo sheets	vinegar
1 small carrot	1 cup olive oil
1/2 leek	1 small cucumber
1 medium onion	1/2 bunch chives, chopped
2 stalks celery	1 large eggplant
1 cup white wine	2 tomatoes
4 cups water	2 medium zucchini
Aromatic herbs of your choice	Salt and pepper

Peel, wash and dice the carrot, leek, onion and celery. Sauté the vegetables in butter and add white wine, water and herbs. Heat to boiling and keep at a low boil for 30 minutes. Strain and reserve 1 cup stock. Make a brunoise (tiny cubes) of the cucumber. In a mixing bowl combine the reserved stock with the tarragon vinegar. Whisk in the olive oil. Season to taste and add the brunoise and the chives.

Cut the phyllo into 2 1/2" x 5" rectangles. Heat the oven to 450 degrees, and adjust the rack to the lower section of the oven. Brush the phyllo lightly with olive oil, cover with a second layer and brush again. Bake until golden brown.

Cut the salmon fillets into 12 rectangles the same dimensions as the phyllo dough. Make the same sized rectangles of the sliced eggplant. Then slice the tomatoes and zucchini into 1/4" slices. Season and sauté all of the vegetables quickly in olive oil and sauté the salmon until it is halfway cooked. Reserve these ingredients on a tray. Brush all the ingredients with some of the tarragon vinaigrette.

Place a rectangle of phyllo on a buttered oven dish, then add a piece of salmon and a slice of eggplant. Then place another rectangle of phyllo, salmon, some sliced tomatoes and another rectangle of phyllo. Finish with the slices of zucchini layered on the top. Repeat this procedure four times. Cook in a 350 degree oven for 5 minutes. Warm up the remaining brunoise and add around the Mille Feuilles on the plates.

Serves 4

Paupiettes of Pacifique Salmon With Vegetables

32 scallops of salmon	4 ounces cooked couscous
4 ounces bean sprouts	4 ounces semolina
2 ounces celery, julienned	3 leeks, white part only
4 ounces carrots, julienned	6 ounces butter
4 ounces diced onion	2 shallots
Salt and pepper	1 cup white wine
2 ounces soy sauce	1 cup fish stock

Pound the slices of salmon gently with meat pounder to a thickness of about 1/4". Refrigerate. In a sauté pan, mix bean sprouts, carrots, celery, onions, soy sauce and 1/2 cup water. Cook covered for 5 minutes. Cool, then mix with couscous and semolina. Place the vegetable mixture in the center of the salmon scallops and wrap in plastic. Steam for 5 minutes. Sauté the shallots and diced leeks in butter. Add the white wine and fish stock and reduce for about 20 minutes, stirring frequently.

To serve: cover the plate with braised leeks, place the paupiettes, sliced in half, on top and garnish with fresh herbs.

Serves 4

Seafood Sausage With Dill Sauce

SEAFOOD SAUSAGE

1 pound salmon	2 tablespoons chives
1 pound shrimp	2 tablespoons parsley
1/2 pound scallops	1 tablespoon tarragon
1 pound grouper	2 teaspoons salt
3 quarts cream	1 tablespoon white pepper
2 tablespoons basil	2 eggs

Grind the salmon, shrimp, scallops and grouper in the food processor. Add eggs, salt, pepper and cream. Blend until mixed. Take out of food processor and put in a bowl. Chop parsley, tarragon, chives and basil and fold into mousse. Wrap in sausage-shaped parchment paper and steam for 20 minutes. Serve with Dill Sauce.

DILL SAUCE

2 cups mayonnaise	1 tablespoon butter
1/2 cup heavy cream	4 tablespoons chopped dill
4 tablespoons chopped shallots	Salt, pepper to taste

Sauté chopped shallots in butter until translucent. Whip mayonnaise and heavy cream together. Add shallots and chopped dill. Blend well. Add salt and pepper to taste. Serve over Seafood Sausage.

Serves 8

RUTH'S CHRIS STEAK HOUSE

"Barbecued" Shrimp

3 pounds jumbo shrimp
1 stick butter
1 stick margarine
1 1/2 ounces Worcestershire
1 1/2 tablespoons black pepper

1/2 teaspoon ground
   rosemary
1/4 teaspoon tabasco
1/2 teaspoon salt
1 large lemon, sliced

Heat oven to 400 degrees. Wash shrimp thoroughly and place (unpeeled) in a large shallow pan. In another saucepan melt butter and margarine. Add Worcestershire, pepper, rosemary, tabasco and salt. Mix thoroughly. Add sliced lemons and mix again. Pour heated sauce over shrimp. Stir well. Place shrimp in oven. Bake for 30 minutes, turning once. When done, shells should be pink, the meat white. Serve with piping hot french bread, salad, corn on the cob and new potatoes.

Serves 6 as an entrée or 10 as an appetizer.

Chipotle Spiced Shrimp With a Salad of Fennel and Radicchio

1 pound shrimp, peeled and
    deveined, tails left on
$1/4$ cup extra virgin olive oil
2 teaspoons chipotle pepper
    puree
1 red onion, sliced
2 fennel, bulb only, sliced
1 tablespoon olive oil
Salt and pepper

2 red pepper, julienned
1 radicchio, julienned
$1/3$ cup vinaigrette
2 tablespoons Italian parsley,
    coarsely chopped
1 teaspoon honey
$1/4$ cup fennel tops,
    chopped

121

In bowl, combine shrimp, oil and pepper puree. Marinate at least 1 hour, covered, in refrigerator. Combine red onion and fennel slices. Toss with olive oil and season with salt and pepper. Place on a cookie sheet. Roast in 350 degree oven for 40-50 minutes, or until lightly caramelized.

Combine roasted fennel and onions with all remaining ingredients. Mix well. Heat a non-stick sauté pan, add shrimp and quickly sauté. Season with salt and pepper. On serving plate, place a generous serving of salad surrounded with shrimp.

Serves 4

Shrimp Cristoforo

1 pound medium shrimp, shelled
2 ounces fresh basil leaves, stemmed
2 1/2 sticks butter, softened
1 teaspoon fresh garlic, chopped
1/4 teaspoon salt
1/8 teaspoon black pepper
3 tablespoons Parmesan cheese
1 tablespoon Romano cheese
1 pound fresh linguine or angel hair pasta

In food processor, chop basil fine (should yield about 3/4 cup). Set aside. Place softened butter in a small mixer bowl. Using electric mixer, whip butter until pliable. Add remaining ingredients (except shrimp), including basil, and mix well. Basil-butter can be used immediately or stored in the refrigerator for 3-4 days.

Cook pasta al dente. Drain well and keep warm. Melt basil-butter in a large skillet over medium heat. Add shrimp and sauté until done, about 2-3 minutes. Serve over hot cooked pasta. Top with additional Parmesan cheese.

Serves 4-6

DAILEY'S

Swordfish Au Poivre

4 10-ounce swordfish steaks, center cut
1/2 cup Dijon mustard
1 tablespoon oil
Scant 1 tablespoon honey

2 tablespoons pink peppercorns
2 tablespoons black pepper-corns
1/2 cup clarified butter

Combine mustard, oil and honey. Spread half of the sauce on a small baking pan. Crush the peppercorns and mix together. Sprinkle half of the mixture over the sauce. Press the fish down onto the pan so that the sauce and pepper adhere. Brush the top of the fish with the remaining sauce and sprinkle the remaining pepper on top. Chill for at least 1 hour.

Melt butter in a large skillet. Sear fish 30 seconds on each side until pepper forms a crust. Transfer to oven and bake at 375 degrees for 15-20 minutes or until done.

Serves 4

Tuna Steaks With Gwo Ba on a Pineapple Vinaigrette

2 6– to 8–ounce tuna steaks	2 ounces oil
1 ounce honey	1/4 cup fresh pineapple
5 ounces Gwo Ba*	2 ounces red wine vinegar
Salt and pepper	2 ounces cream

Rub the tuna steaks with a light coat of honey. Lightly season with salt and pepper. Press the steaks firmly into the Gwo Ba so that the top of the steak is covered. Heat the oil in a non-stick pan. When the oil is smoking, add the steaks carefully Gwo Ba side down. Cook for 30-45 seconds or until the Gwo Ba is crisp. Reduce heat, flip steaks and finish cooking.

Peel, core and dice the pineapple. Heat the 1/4 cup pineapple with vinegar and boil for 5 minutes. Add cream and cook another 2 minutes. Puree in a blender or food processor for 10 seconds. Serve under the tuna.

*Gwo Ba – "sizzling rice" – can be found in oriental markets.

Serves 2

Desserts

Desserts

Amaretto Fingers: Affairs to Remember Caterers

Bahamian Bananas: Indigo Coastal Grill

William's Bananas Foster: Rupert's Catering

Brutti Ma Buoni: Bice

Bread Pudding with Whiskey Sauce: Ruth's Chris
Steak House

Rice Pudding: The Coach and Six

Chocolate Pecan Torte: Delectables

Chocolate Truffle Pâté: My Friend's Place

Chocolate Walnut Bourbon Pie: Stouffer Waverly Hotel

Creme Brulee in Puff Dough: The Ritz-Carlton Buckhead

Peach Blackberry Cobbler: Georgia Grille

Peaches and Cream Tart: Delectables

Peaches 'N Cream Cheesecake: The Olive Garden

Pumpkin Cheesecake: The Peasant Restaurants

White Chocolate Cheesecake with Fresh Berries:
Hyatt Regency Atlanta

Amaretto Fingers

³/₄ cup shortening
4 1–ounce squares
   unsweetened chocolate
2 cups sugar
1 ¹/₄ cups all–purpose flour
1 cup chopped almonds

1 cup almond paste
1 teaspoon baking powder
1 teaspoon salt
4 eggs
Garnish: white chocolate

Heat oven to 350 degrees. Heat shortening and chocolate in 3 quart saucepan over low heat until melted. Remove from heat. Stir in remaining ingredients. Spread in greased 13" x 9" x 2" rectangular pan. Bake until slightly pulling away from sides of pan (about 30 minutes). Do not over bake. Let cool. Cut into bars. Drizzle with melted white chocolate.

Serves 10

Bahamian Bananas

4 tablespoons butter
4 bananas, sliced lengthwise
1/3 cup turbinado sugar
1 cup heavy cream

3 tablespoons key lime or
regular lime juice
Garnish per serving:
2 tablespoons turbinado
sugar, lime wedges

Heat butter in sauté pan until bubbling. Sprinkle the bananas with half of the sugar and sauté in butter until they are brown on both sides and the sugar is beginning to caramelize. Set the bananas aside and keep warm.

In another pan, bring the cream to a boil and reduce by one third. Add remaining sugar, reduce heat and simmer until the sugar is incorporated. Add the lime juice, stirring, and cook until thickened. Place bananas on warmed plates and drizzle sauce on top. Garnish.

Serves 4

William's Bananas Foster

6–8 ripe bananas
2 tablespoons unsalted
butter or margarine
4 tablespoons light brown
sugar
$1/2$ teaspoon ground cinnamon
$1/2$ teaspoon ground ginger
$1/2$ teaspoon salt
1 teaspoon vanilla extract or

$1/2$ fresh vanilla bean, split
2 teaspoons grated zest (may
use orange, lemon or
grapefruit)
$1/2$ cup dark rum
Splash orange liqueur or
triple sec
6 portions vanilla bean
ice cream

Over medium heat, warm a 10" or 12" skillet (not teflon), with the butter and brown sugar. Cook the butter and sugar for about 2 minutes. Add the cinnamon, ginger, salt, vanilla and zest. Cook only 30–45 seconds more and add the bananas, basting them in the sauce.

Away from the heat source, add the rum (if using a gas stove this is when the flames appear or if using an electric stove strike a long fireplace match to the pan for flames). Return to the heat source. Stir the pan briefly, and extinguish the flames with the liqueur. Spoon the ice cream on top, divide into 6 portions and serve immediately.

Serves 6

BICE

Brutti Ma Buoni

(UGLY BUT GOOD)

¹/₂ cup egg whites
  (approximately 5)
1 cup sugar

¹/₂ cup hazelnut pieces
¹/₂ teaspoon lemon juice

Whip sugar and egg whites until firm peaks form. Add lemon juice and hazelnuts. Drop mixture by the teaspoonful onto foil lined cookie sheet. Bake at 100 degrees overnight (8-10 hours).

Serves 8

Bread Pudding With Whiskey Sauce

6 tablespoons butter, softened
³/₄ cup sugar
3 large eggs, beaten
2 cups milk
¹/₂ teaspoon nutmeg
1 teaspoon cinnamon
1 teaspoon vanilla
¹/₈ teaspoon salt
¹/₂ cup raisins

4 cups French bread cubes

Whiskey Sauce:
1 stick butter
1 cup sugar
1 large egg, beaten
¹/₄ cup 80–proof bourbon whiskey

Heat oven to 350 degrees. In a large bowl, cream together butter and sugar. Add eggs, milk, nutmeg, cinnamon, vanilla and salt. Mix thoroughly. By hand, fold in ¹/₄ cup of the raisins and stir well. Add bread cubes and stir again. Let mixture stand for 5 minutes to allow bread to soak up some of the liquid. Pour into a well–greased large shallow baking pan. Top with remaining raisins. Push raisins down into bread mixture. Let stand 20 more minutes. Bake uncovered for 45 minutes.

Top with the whiskey sauce: Melt butter and sugar in the top of a double boiler. Add beaten egg gradually with whisk. Remove from heat, cool slightly. Add bourbon and mix thoroughly. Pour warm sauce over pudding and serve.

Serves 8-10

Rice Pudding

2 cups milk
1/2 cup half & half
1/3 cup uncooked rice
1/4 cup sugar
1/8 teaspoon salt

1/4 teaspoon vanilla extract
1 cup heavy cream
1/4 cup raisins
1/2 teaspoon cinnamon

In top of double boiler, combine milk, half & half, rice, sugar, salt and vanilla. Bring to a boil. Reduce heat to medium. Cook, stirring frequently, until rice is tender and sauce has thickened (about 40 minutes). Let cool. In medium bowl, whip heavy cream until thick. Saving enough whipped cream for garnish, fold whipped cream into rice mixture. Fold in raisins and cinnamon. Pour into 4 8-ounce cups. Top each with reserved whipped cream. Brown lightly under broiler.

Serves 4

Chocolate Pecan Torte

4 ounces bittersweet chocolate, melted	4 ounces unsalted butter
8 ounces pecans	3 large eggs
3/4 cup sugar, divided	1 tablespoon espresso powder
	2 tablespoons coffee liqueur

Dissolve the espresso powder in the coffee liqueur. Preheat oven to 350 degrees. Grease an 8" cake pan and line with parchment paper. In the work bowl of a food processor, grind the pecans with 1/4 cup of the sugar. Place in medium sized bowl and set aside.

Place melted chocolate, butter, eggs and espresso liquid into the work bowl. Pulse until blended. Add the remaining 1/2 cup of sugar and incorporate. Pour chocolate mixture over the pecan mixture and blend with a whisk until smooth. Pour into prepared pan and bake for 25 minutes.

Remove from oven and cool on a wire rack. When completely cooled pour chocolate ganache (recipe follows) over the torte and garnish with pecan halves that have been dipped halfway into ganache. Ring the outer edge with the dipped pecans. Transfer to a cake plate.

CHOCOLATE GANACHE FOR TORTE

8 ounces bittersweet chocolate, chopped	4 ounces heavy cream
	1 teaspoon espresso powder

Dissolve the espresso powder in the cream and heat almost to boiling. Remove from heat and add the chocolate. Whisk to melt the chocolate. Pour over the cooled torte, letting ganache run over and down the sides. Use extra ganache to dip pecan halves.

Serves 8

Cameron Wood

137

Chocolate Truffle Pâté

6 ounces semisweet chocolate	2–3 tablespoons almond or
6 ounces bittersweet chocolate	orange liqueur
1 ²/₃ cups heavy cream	1 ¹/₄ cups blanched
5 tablespoons butter	almonds, chopped fine

Combine and melt both chocolates in the top of a double boiler over hot water. Add butter, stirring until melted. Add the cream, and heat until scalded. Remove from heat. Stir briskly until the chocolate cools and thickens. Add liqueur and nuts. Spoon into a small crock and press a piece of plastic wrap onto the surface of pâté to keep it from hardening. Chill.

When ready to serve, remove plastic wrap and serve with an assortment of English biscuits, shortbread cookies and fresh fruit such as apples, pears and strawberries.

Serves 10

Chocolate Walnut Bourbon Pie

2/3 cup raisins
1/2 cup bourbon
1 cup unsifted flour*
1/4 teaspoon salt*
4 tablespoons butter*
1 1/2 tablespoons shortening, chilled*
3–4 tablespoon cold water*
1 cup brown sugar
1/2 cup sugar

1 teaspoon flour
1/8 teaspoon salt
3 eggs
1/2 teaspoon vanilla extract
3 tablespoons butter, melted
1/2 cup heavy cream
1/2 cup chocolate chips
1 cup chopped walnuts

* Or use 1 9" pie shell

Soak raisins in bourbon for 30 minutes to one hour. Raisins will soak up most of bourbon. Pour off extra bourbon.

Make pie shell: mix salt and flour together. Cut cold butter and shortening into small chunks and stir into flour mixture. Add cold water slowly and stir as mixture becomes dough. Roll out dough and press into 9" pie pan. Chill crust in the refrigerator for 30 minutes before baking.

Mix together the brown sugar, sugar, flour, salt, eggs and vanilla. Add melted butter and heavy cream. Put walnuts, raisins and chocolate chips in pie shell. Pour filling mixture on top. Bake at 375 degrees for 30-35 minutes, or until the top of the pie turns light brown.

Serves 8

Creme Brulee in Puff Dough

6 ounces + 1 tablespoon sugar	1 sheet frozen puff dough
12 egg yolks	1 sheet parchment
3/4 ounce cornstarch	1/2 pint fresh raspberries
1 vanilla bean	1/2 pound beans (these are
3 cups heavy cream	for weight only – see
	recipe)

Whisk together sugar, egg yolks and cornstarch over double boiler until the mixture is hot, taking care not to curdle the eggs. Bring vanilla bean and heavy cream to a boil, and add to egg yolk mixture. Whisk together well. Cool in ice bath. Set aside.

Roll pastry out to 1 1/2 times original size. Cut pastry into a circle 6" in diameter. Line a 4" cake ring with pastry. Place parchment on top. Fill with beans (this keeps dough thin and crispy). Bake in a 375 degree oven for 15 minutes. Let cool.

Fill with creme brulee and top with berries. Sprinkle with granulated sugar. Caramelize under a broiler. Serve with raspberry puree.

Serves 6

Peach Blackberry Cobbler

2 1/2 cups flour	4 cups fresh blackberries
1/2 teaspoon baking soda	1/2 cup sugar
1/2 teaspoon salt	1 teaspoon vanilla
4 ounces shortening	Topping:
3/4 cup milk	1/2 cup sugar
8 cups fresh peach slices	2 ounces butter

Make pastry: place flour, soda and salt in mixing bowl. Add shortening and combine until mixture resembles large grains. Stir in milk just to mix. Turn out onto board and gently roll into rectangle to cover a 9″ x 12″ baking pan.

For filling: combine peaches, blackberries, sugar and vanilla. Place in 9″ x 12″ pan. Cover with rolled out pastry. Sprinkle top of pastry with sugar and dot with butter. Bake at 400 degrees for 20-25 minutes or until pastry begins to brown and is crisp.

Serves 8

Peaches and Cream Tart

CRUST

1/3 cup almonds, finely ground	1/4 teaspoon baking powder
1 1/2 cups all-purpose flour	1/2 cup butter, softened
1/3 cup sugar	1/2 teaspoon almond extract
1/2 teaspoon salt	

Pulse all dry ingredients in food processor until well mixed. Add butter and almond extract and pulse until a crumbly mixture is formed. Press mixture into a lightly greased 10″ tart pan.

FILLING

8 ripe, firm peaches, peeled, thinly sliced	1/4 cup sugar
1 teaspoon lemon juice	1/2 teaspoon cinnamon
2 teaspoons peach liqueur	2 egg yolks
	1 cup sour cream

Place lemon juice, liqueur, sugar and cinnamon in bowl and mix well. Toss in peach slices and mix well. Arrange slices in concentric circles over crust. Reserve juices. Bake in a 400 degree oven for 15 minutes. Remove from oven. Mix reserved juices in bowl with egg yolks and sour cream. Pour over peach tart. Sprinkle with cinnamon. Bake for an additional 15 minutes. Let cool.

Serves 8

Peaches 'n Cream Cheesecake

1 egg	1 teaspoon all-purpose flour
1/3 cup sugar	1 teaspoon vanilla
1/4 teaspoon vanilla	1 cup sour cream
1/4 cup all-purpose flour	1/4 cup peach liqueur
1/4 teaspoon baking powder	or peach schnapps or
Pinch salt	reserved peach juice
2 tablespoons water	2 cups peaches, canned or
2 pounds cream cheese	fresh, sliced
1 cup sugar	1 pint whipping cream
4 eggs	

To make sponge cake base: preheat oven to 375 degrees. Grease base of 10″ springform pan. Beat 1 egg in a 1 1/2 quart bowl with mixer on high for 4 minutes, so it forms a thick yellow foam. Mix in the 1/3 cup of sugar on low speed until smooth. Add the 1/4 teaspoon vanilla, the 1/4 cup flour, baking powder, salt and water. Mix on low speed until fully blended. Pour into springform pan, roll around until level. Bake 16-18 minutes on lowest rack. Let cool to room temperature.

For cheesecake filling: reduce oven heat to 325 degrees. With mixer on high, mix cream cheese, sugar, eggs and flour. Add vanilla, sour cream and peach liqueur and mix on medium speed to a smooth consistency. Fold in peach slices carefully, distributing evenly. Pour cheesecake filling into cooled sponge cake base. Bake 70 minutes on lower oven rack. Turn oven off, leave door ajar, and allow cake to remain in oven for 40 minutes. Cool in refrigerator. Top with fresh whipped cream.

Serves 8

Pumpkin Cheesecake

3 pounds cream cheese, room
    temperature
2 2/3 cups sugar
6 extra large eggs
2 teaspoons vanilla extract
1 3/4 cups cooked pumpkin
1 tablespoon cinnamon
2 teaspoons nutmeg

1/2 teaspoon ginger
1 10" graham cracker
    crust or 3 cups
    graham cracker crumbs
8 ounces melted unsalted
    butter
1/4 cup sugar
1 tablespoon cinnamon

Line bottom of 10" x 3" cheesecake pan (not springform) with parchment. Beat cream cheese with mixer until soft. Add sugar and continue beating until all lumps disappear, scraping bowl often. Add eggs and vanilla and stir into batter. Add pumpkin, cinnamon, nutmeg and ginger. Stir into batter. Make crust. Combine ingredients and press into bottom of prepared pan. Add batter. Place pan inside larger roasting pan. Fill bottom pan with water to 1 1/2". Bake at 350 degrees for 3 hours. Refrigerate overnight.

Dip pan in hot water for 10 seconds. Place a cardboard circle on top of pan. Invert and tap pan on side of table. Cake should slip right out. Invert again onto serving platter. Top each serving with 1/2 cup of whipped cream.

Serves 8

White Chocolate Cheesecake With Fresh Berries

1 ¹/₄ cups graham cracker crumbs	10 ounces white chocolate
¹/₄ cup sugar	2 ounces raspberry liqueur
¹/₃ cup melted butter	1 pint blueberries
1 ¹/₂ pounds cream cheese	1 pint raspberries
1 cup sugar	Topping:
3 eggs	24 ounces sour cream
	³/₄ cup sugar

Grease springform or cheesecake pan. Combine in bowl the crumbs, sugar and butter. Pat down into the bottom of prepared pan. Bake in 350 degree oven for 8 minutes. Remove pan from oven.

In double boiler, melt and cool the white chocolate, then set aside. In large mixer bowl on medium high speed, cream together the cream cheese and the sugar. Add the eggs one at a time, incorporating well. Add the white chocolate. Fold in the raspberry liqueur and the fresh berries. Pour into prepared crust. Place cheesecake pan in water bath (larger pan filled with water to come up 1 ¹/₂" on sides). Bake at 350 degrees for 70 minutes, or until set in center.

For topping, whip together the sour cream and sugar. Pour over top of cake. Bake for an additional 5-10 minutes. Refrigerate cake overnight.

Serves 8

$\mathcal{I}$ndex

149

Margaret Norman is an Atlanta native with a keen interest in both the Atlanta Community Food Bank and her own kitchen. She lives with her husband and two children in Lithonia, Georgia.